Ten Years of Hippocampus Press:
2000–2010

Ten Years of Hippocampus Press:
2000–2010

Derrick Hussey, S. T. Joshi,
and David E. Schultz

Hippocampus Press
_____

New York

Published by Hippocampus Press
P.O. Box 641, New York, NY 10156
http://www.hippocampuspress.com

Cover design by Barbara Briggs Silbert.
Hippocampus Press logo designed by Anastasia Damianakos.

ISBN 978-0-9844802-8-9

Foreword

Derrick Hussey

It is remarkable to consider that we stand at ten years of Hippocampus Press as a direct result of a conversation between some friends at dinner over a decade ago. The suggestion was put forward to start an independent press, taking up the baton from our predecessors in Lovecraftian publishing who had largely gotten away from a vigorous publishing schedule. In a sense the press can trace its roots further back, to my involvement in the amateur press association, the Esoteric Order of Dagon. But the leap from creating amateur magazines, intended for a few, to publishing books intended for a wider audience was a defining moment, a phase change.

Since that time we have committed in excess of nine million words to paper, on more than twenty-three thousand pages. Although in the eyes of the mainstream Hippocampus Press is still, perhaps rightly, considered an amateur outfit, we have had more than our share of successes. The projects we undertake are continually growing. Over the decade now passed, our procedures have become relatively streamlined and, thankfully, we have learned from our several missteps how to avoid, for the most part, their recurrence.

The press has been successful heretofore in the meaningful sense of having been able to continue our activities, and to grow both the size and number of our projects. Financial aspects have not been overly problematic, perhaps a testament to the accuracy with which we anticipate the needs and wants of the worldwide community of enthusiasts who form our loyal customer base. Happily, we have not been constrained only to release those works that stand to be a commercial success; among our projects, in the past and going forward, are many that, beyond being of interest to us personally, stood out as needing to be done for the benefit of the field. In recent years we have broadened our scope to include publishing new authors whose writing appeals to us in one way or another; collecting works that are of intense interest to a minute section of the reading public; and launching scholarly print journals at a time when these seem to be fading from the scene.

One of the enduring strengths of Hippocampus has been our willingness to undertake highly specialized projects, with no greater determinant than our own taste in Lovecraftiana. From the beginning the focus has been on books of merit that, without our intervention, might never grace a bookshelf. Our first publication took an entire year to produce, coming as it did with the birthing pains of the press itself, as we learned how to achieve our intention. In ten years we have gone from this snail's pace to that of a slightly fleeter snail, perhaps. But in our wake is a considerable body of literature, numbering among itself some several works which are reckoned to be milestones in their field. The team that forms our core is small, and separated by considerable distance. David E. Schultz is in Milwaukee; S. T. Joshi is in Seattle, and Barbara Silbert, Anastasia, and I are in New York. At no time have all the principals been gathered together in one place. I am not certain when such a gathering, certainly to be hoped for, will ever be consummated. Each of us has any number of other concerns and interests that take up the majority of our lives. For my part, I am grateful to have been afforded the opportunity to work with these fine people, together with authors and editors; artists, printers, and booksellers; agencies and estates; for the benefit of our readers worldwide.

W. Paul Cook, an influence on my publishing aspirations, adopted as the motto of his press, "For Love Alone." Unable to adhere strictly to this lofty principle, it nevertheless can be reported that these ten years and the stack of publications to our name can rightly be ascribed to love of the field *first*, alloyed with an aspect of professionalism, mindful of the compromises made for the sake of practicality. Our catalogue is largely of a piece, accurately reflecting a single publishing aesthetic. Our house style, we hope, exemplifies a uniformly high degree of scholarly and technical exactingness. This listing of our works, or catalogue of sins if you prefer, accurately charts our progress through the past ten years. Further, it is anticipated to form a bellwether of the future. Those projects that would seem naturally to follow, and which would be glaring in their absence, are probably scheduled for a year or two hence. God willing, we shall be able to continue doing what we do.

My Years with Hippocampus Press

S. T. Joshi

It must have been sometime in 1999 when, at a dinner of the "New Kalem Club"—an informal group of Lovecraft devotees who gathered at O'Reilly's Irish Pub on 31st Street in Manhattan once a month or so to shoot the bull and down a pint of Guinness (some of the more faint-hearted members settled for Bass Ale)—that I leaned over to Derrick Hussey and said, "How'd you like to start a new small press?"

I will be frank: my purpose was in some sense self-serving. Marc Michaud's Necronomicon Press was undergoing a certain turmoil because of Marc's personal difficulties, and I felt the need for another small press to take up the slack. By that time, my horizons had expanded from the narrow world of Lovecraft scholarship to the broader study of weird fiction, and I felt that a press that could take advantage of the burgeoning interest in Lovecraft and other weird writers, both "classic" and modern, could serve an important purpose.

Back in 1999, a number of needs in the study of Lovecraft were still unmet. His collected poetry had not been issued (I had prepared such an edition, initially scheduled for publication by Arkham House, then by Necronomicon Press, and finally released by Night Shade Books in 2001), his collected essays had not been assembled, his immense body of letters remained largely unpublished; and, of course, there was the ongoing need to advance Lovecraft scholarship—a task that was being hindered by the virtual cessation of the flagship journal in the field, *Lovecraft Studies.* (Over the next several years, a few more issues of *Lovecraft Studies* did appear—one published by Hippocampus Press—but the journal finally collapsed in 2004.)

In addition, there remained many significant works of weird fiction—both novels and collections of stories—whose intrinsic merit, and whose influence upon Lovecraft's own work, demanded their reprinting. Although such publishers as Ash-Tree Press and Tartarus Press were then engaging in a course of reprinting many weird classics, these were for the most part in the tradition of the Victorian ghost story, which did not influence Lovecraft significantly and therefore would not have any direct appeal to Lovecraftians. (Tartarus Press began as an imprint for restoring the work of Arthur Machen into print.) So the outlook for a new press seemed bright.

In fact, I recall mentioning to Derrick, "If you begin a press, I can guarantee that I myself can supply you with enough titles to keep it operating indefinitely." This was not spoken out of arrogance, or for the purpose of making

Hippocampus Press a private imprint of my own; it was simply a recognition that the press could fill a niche in the realm of small-press publishing that was currently not being met by other imprints, and that, after twenty or more years of research, I was in a position to prepare editions of Lovecraft and other writers that could keep a small press busy for years. Whether such a press could actually keep afloat financially by issuing such editions was a question for another day.

Derrick, who had recently left a position at the New York office of Routledge and seemed to be looking for something to fill up his time, readily assented. I was aware that he had a certain modicum of capital behind him—an essential requirement for a small press, since it was unlikely that our first several titles would be blockbusters. As our first title, I offered my extensively annotated edition of *Supernatural Horror in Literature*—an edition that had actually been assembled all the way back in 1981 (based on an initial expression of interest by Greenwood Press that was subsequently withdrawn). My friend and colleague David E. Schultz had done a preliminary layout of the book, for the purpose of estimating how big it might be, and Derrick felt satisfied that the result was a book worth publishing. So the first Hippocampus Press title slipped unobtrusively into print in the year 2000.

My recollection is that the book was fairly well received; I have no figures on how well it sold, but it did eventually get reprinted. It took us a full year to prepare another volume for the press, and this too was a book that had long been delayed—an annotated edition of the corrected text of Lovecraft's "The Shadow out of Time." The spectacular discovery of Lovecraft's original manuscript, among the effects of a woman in Hawaii, created a furore in 1994. I was the first scholar to be allowed access to the manuscript, and in February of 1994 I prepared a corrected text; but that text sat for years while legal and other difficulties were resolved.

Since then, Hippocampus Press has published books on a seemingly wide array of subjects, but I believe most or all of them can boil down to a few broad rubrics: 1) material by or about H. P. Lovecraft; 2) material by Lovecraft's friends and colleagues; 3) material that may have influenced Lovecraft; and 4) original work by leading authors of weird fiction or by promising newcomers.

It was not long after the publication of the first two Hippocampus titles that I broached the subject of publishing Lovecraft's collected essays. There still remained a few essays by Lovecraft that had not been published at all, while many others were scattered in a multitude of small-press volumes. The framework of what became the five-volume *Collected Essays* (2004–06) was suggested by my edition of Lovecraft's *Miscellaneous Writings* (Arkham House, 1995), where a topical or thematic division of the essays was presented, rather than a strictly chronological arrangement. And yet, this division itself was based upon a provisional arrangement of Lovecraft's complete works that I had devised as early as 1980, as I was working on the first edition of my bibliography of Lovecraft (1981). In that sense, the *Collected Essays* constitutes virtually the final instalment of what I had then envisioned as a 13-volume *Collected Works of H. P. Lovecraft.* (I say "virtually" because an annotated edition of Lovecraft's revisions and collaborations—which would probably extend to two volumes—has yet to be assembled. I am now contemplating such an edition.)

Of course, the last frontier in the publication of Lovecraft's work is his letters. Necronomicon Press had made a start by issuing batches of letters to individual correspondents (Henry Kuttner, Richard F. Searight, Robert Bloch) in the early 1990s, and Hippocampus Press followed up that program by publishing the letters to Alfred Galpin (2003) and Rheinhart Kleiner (2005), edited by David E. Schultz and myself. At that point our horizons expanded, and we wondered whether the entirety of Lovecraft's letters could be issued in book form (as opposed to electronically), with exhaustive annotations. Our first venture in this regard was the massive two-volume edition of Lovecraft's letters to August Derleth (2008), followed—after years of legal and logistical difficulties—with the even more massive two-volume edition of Lovecraft's letters to Robert E. Howard (2009). These titles, in effect, constitute the first four volumes of what promise to be approximately 25 volumes of Lovecraft letters, and we hope to issue a two-volume edition of the joint correspondence of Lovecraft and Clark Ashton Smith in 2011.

Mention of Smith brings to mind that we have engaged in substantial work in Smith studies. My edition of Smith's juvenile novel, *The Black Diamonds* (2002), was again based on work that had been done years ago: in 1979–81, Marc Michaud and I had catalogued Smith's papers and manuscripts for the John Hay Library of Brown University, and among those papers was *The Black Diamonds*. The manuscript was a fearful mess, and it took me some time to ascertain that it constituted a full version (minus a few pages) of the first draft and several short attempts at subsequent drafts (these drafts have not been published); it took still more time to decipher Smith's youthful chirography and transcribe the text. After the book was issued, Dr. W. C. Farmer, a late colleague of Smith's, announced that he had the two missing pages of the manuscript, along with another, somewhat shorter juvenile novel, *The Sword of Zagan,* as well as other material. These texts were issued in 2004. We also issued Smith's *Last Oblivion* (2002), a selection of his best fantastic poetry, which set the stage for the three-volume edition of Smith's *Complete Poems and Translations* (2007–08), an edition that David E. Schultz had been working on since the 1980s. We also published a noteworthy collection of articles about Smith, *The Freedom of Fantastic Things* (2006), edited by Scott Connors, now the leading Smith scholar.

Lovecraft's colleagues have fared well at Hippocampus Press, with editions of the writings of R. H. Barlow (2002), Samuel Loveman (2004), Donald Wandrei (*Sanctity and Sin* [2008], an expansion of Wandrei's *Collected Poems* [Necronomicon Press, 1988]), Edith Miniter (2008), and a number of others. Hippocampus publications of George Sterling, the California poet who was the early mentor of Clark Ashton Smith, are a result of my own devoted interest in this much-neglected writer. I was pleased to issue a volume of Sterling's weird verse, *The Thirst of Satan* (2003), which will set the stage for a massive three-volume edition of Sterling's collected poetry and verse drama, probably to be issued in 2011. Schultz and I also edited the joint correspondence of Sterling and Smith (*The Shadow of the Unattained*, 2005).

Scholarship on Lovecraft has been enhanced by the re-establishment of a journal devoted to his life and work, *The Lovecraft Annual* (2007f.), as well as a volume of Robert H. Waugh's scintillating essays, *The Monster in the Mirror: Looking for H. P. Lovecraft* (2006). Another collection of Waugh's essays is forthcoming. Within this rubric might be considered the highly innovative volume *Lovecraft's New York Circle: The Kalem Club, 1924–1927* (2006), assembled largely by Mara Kirk Hart (the daughter of George Kirk) with minimal assistance by me. This volume contains substantial literary material by the various core members of the Kalem Club (Rheinhart Kleiner, Arthur Leeds, Frank Belknap Long, Samuel Loveman, Everett McNeil, James F. Morton) and is preceded by the fascinating "Kalem Letters"—a batch of letters by George Kirk written to his fiancée, Lucile Dvorak, which provides an unprecedented first-hand glimpse of the Kalems in New York. Kenneth W. Faig, Jr.'s *The Unknown Lovecraft* (2009) will, I hope, finally bring recognition to this pioneering Lovecraft scholar for the invaluable work he has done over the past thirty years or more.

The fostering of scholarship has been an important objective at Hippocampus Press. We are well aware that there are fewer and fewer outlets for the study of weird fiction, as many academic publishers that formerly published this material are now cutting back in the wake of budget cuts. Benjamin Szumskyj's admirable anthology of essays on Robert E. Howard, *Two-Gun Bob* (2006), along with such of my own volumes as *Primal Sources: Essays on H. P. Lovecraft* (2003), *The Evolution of the Weird Tale* (2004), and *Classics and Contemporaries* (2009), have been generally well received; and I was pleased to lend some assistance to Rosemary Pardoe in a splendid volume of criticism of M. R. James, *Warnings to the Curious* (2007). In a somewhat related vein, our founding of *Dead Reckonings* (2007f.), a review journal devoted to weird fiction—based in large part upon the successful *Necrofile* (1991–99), issued by Necronomicon Press—has resulted in substantive analysis of contemporary work in the field.

The press has also done important work in another area of weird fiction that tends to be given short shrift—weird poetry. The volumes by Barlow, Loveman, and Wandrei, cited above, contain substantial amounts of poetry, and the recent publication of Nora May French's collected poetry, *The Outer*

Gate (2009), connects with the press's interest in Smith, Sterling, and poetry. The press's first work of original creative writing was R. Nemo Hill's *The Strange Music of Erich Zann* (2004), a poetic extrapolation from Lovecraft's "The Music of Erich Zann." H. L. Mencken's *Collected Poems* (2009) may seem far out of the scope of Hippocampus Press, but it reflects our ongoing interest in poetry and my own personal interest in the work of the iconoclast from Baltimore. And the publication of Donald Sidney-Fryer's immense *Atlantis Fragments* (2008)—a compendium of his three volumes of *Songs and Sonnets Atlantean*, some of the finest weird poetry and prose-poetry written since the heyday of Clark Ashton Smith—represents the culmination of Sidney-Fryer's illustrious career as a creative artist.

The publication of my revised edition of *Lovecraft's Library: A Catalogue* (2002) may have triggered the "Lovecraft's Library" series, in which novels and tales that inspired Lovecraft, or in some cases were simply appreciated by him, are reprinted. The series was initiated even before the publication of *Lovecraft's Library* by Stefan Dziemianowicz's edition of A. Merritt's *The Metal Monster* (2002), but got underway in earnest with the issuance of Herbert Gorman's *The Place Called Dagon* (2003). In 2007 we released the first Hippocampus Press "double," an imitation of the format of the old "Ace doubles," where two novels were printed in one book. In this way, several short novels could be issued together, since there still remain numerous titles that Lovecraftians will wish to read for their possible influence on Lovecraft's seminal tales.

The most exciting development at Hippocampus Press—and one that we never envisioned when we first began the press—was the issuance of new creative work by leading contemporary writers and promising new voices. As mentioned, R. Nemo Hill's booklet was our first such venture, but the program gathered steam with the issuance of *The Fungal Stain and Other Dreams* (2006), by W. H. Pugmire, a writer whose Lovecraftian-related work I have long admired. We have subsequently published distinguished work by both veterans (Ramsey Campbell's *Inconsequential Tales*, 2008; Donald R. Burleson's *Wait for the Thunder: Stories for a Stormy Night*, 2010) and newcomers (Philip Haldeman's *Shadow Coast*, 2007; Jonathan Thomas's *Midnight Call and Other Stories*, 2008; Joseph S. Pulver, Sr.'s *Blood Will Have Its Season*, 2009; Michael Aronovitz's *Seven Deadly Pleasures*, 2009). We are thrilled that most of these volumes have been well received by critics and readers. Our promotion of noteworthy contributions to Lovecraft's "Cthulhu Mythos" began with Robert M. Price's edition of *Tales out of Dunwich* (2005) and continued through Franklyn Searight's *Lair of the Dreamer* (2007), Adam Niswander's pair of novels, *The Hound Hunters* (2009) and *The War of the Whisperers* (2009), and Robert M. Price's edition of *The Tindalos Cycle* (2010).

As Hippocampus Press continues its publications in its several different lines—ranging from my two-volume biography, *I Am Providence: The Life and*

Times of H. P. Lovecraft (2010), to original fiction by Jonathan Thomas and Joseph S. Pulver, Sr., poetry by Fred Phillips, continuing editions of Lovecraft's letters, and much other work, I think it can safely be said that the press has established itself as one of the most vital imprints in the field of weird fiction, and can look forward to many years of critical success. But it is the devotion of its many readers that will carry the press into the future, and we hope to continue earning that devotion by the publications we hope to issue in the coming years.

Publications of Hippocampus Press
2000–2010

1. H. P. LOVECRAFT. *The Annotated Supernatural Horror in Literature*. Edited by S. T. Joshi. 2000 (rpt. 2004). 172 pp.

    Contents. Preface; Introduction; Supernatural Horror in Literature, by H. P. Lovecraft; Appendix: The Favorite Weird Stories of H P. Lovecraft; Notes; Bibliography of Authors and Works; Index.

    Notes. Cover illustration by Vrest Orton from the *Recluse* 1 (1927). First printing, 1000 copies plus unspecified overrun, Morris Publishing, Kearney, NE. Rpt November 2004 as a print-on-demand (POD) book. A work Joshi compiled as early as 1981 but for which he could not find a publisher. The text of Lovecraft's essay has been printed accurately here for the first time, as Joshi has collated all previous publications, including the original publication in the *Recluse* (1927) and the serialization in the *Fantasy Fan* (1933–35). Joshi has added extensive commentary and a substantial primary and secondary bibliography for all authors and works discussed in the treatise. A new and updated edition is forthcoming.

2. H. P. LOVECRAFT. *The Shadow out of Time.* Edited by S. T. Joshi and David E. Schultz. 2001 (rpt. 2003). 136 pp.

    Contents. Introduction; The Shadow out of Time, by H. P. Lovecraft; APPENDIX: Notes to "The Shadow out of Time"; Early draft; Notes; Textual Notes.

    Notes. Cover illustration by Howard V. Brown. First printing, 1000 copies plus unspecified overrun; Morris Publishing. Reprint issued simultaneously in 2003 with two competing POD companies, Booksurge and Lightning Source, to compare quality and service. Booksurge POD edition was taken out of print sometime later, and only a handful of this variant state were circulated. Booksurge edition distinguished by matte finish on cover, while all Lightning Source paperbacks have a glossy finish on covers. Lightning Source POD and Morris Publishing editions were available simultaneously for a time.

    A landmark publication of the original ms. of Lovecraft's story, which was believed lost until it surfaced in 1994. Joshi was the first scholar to be allowed to consult the text, which he did in February 1994; but various logistical delays prevented the publication of the edition until 2001. The text, which contains at least 400 textual corrections from the minimally corrected edition in *The Dunwich Horror and Others* (Arkham House, 1984), is exhaustively annotated, with textual variants and a discussion of the finding of the ms. by John H. Stanley, a curator at the John Hay Library, Brown University.

3. *Studies in Weird Fiction 25.* Edited by S. T. Joshi. Summer 2001. 40 pp.

    Contents. From Haunted Rose Gardens to Lurking Wendigos: Liminal and Wild Places in M. R. James and Algernon Blackwood, by Linda J. Holland-Toll; Hawthorne, Hitchcock, and the Fine Women of *Blithedale* and *Psycho*, by Marilyn Knight; Gesturing Toward the Infinite: Clark Ashton Smith and Modernism, by Scott Connors; The Weird Verse of Christopher Brennan, by Phillip A. Ellis; Things from the Sea: The Early Weird Fiction of Frank Belknap Long, by S. T. Joshi; Correspondence.

    Notes. Cover by Robert H. Knox. Back cover photograph of Clark Ashton Smith in 1912 by Bianca Conti. Two hundred copies plus unspecified overrun. A long-delayed issue of a magazine first published (1986f.) by Necronomicon Press. Awkwardly, Necronomicon Press itself issued its own No. 25 (Summer 2003), followed by the final issue, No. 27 (Spring 2005).

4. *Lovecraft Studies 42–43.* Edited by S. T. Joshi. Autumn 2001. 76 pp.

    Contents. Editorial; The Book, by H. P. Lovecraft; The Book of "The Book," by Michael Cisco; H. P. Lovecraft: Reluctant American Modernist, by Steven J. Mariconda; H. P. Lovecraft in Florida, by Stephen J. Jordan; Antique Dreams: Marblehead and Lovecraft's Kingsport, by Donovan K. Loucks; A Note on "The Book," by Donald R. Burleson; The Problem with Solving: Implications for Sherlock Holmes and Lovecraft Narrators, by Deborah D'Agati; The Lurker at the Threshold of Interpretation: Hoax *Necronomicons* and Paratextual Noise by Dan Clore; The Mirror in the House: Looking at the Horror of Looking at the Horror, by P. S. Owens; Review.

    Notes. Cover by Jason Eckhardt. Two hundred copies plus unspecified overrun. Another long-delayed issue of a journal first published (1979f.) by Necronomicon Press. The latter published two further issues, No. 44 (2004) and No. 45 (Spring 2005). The journal was succeeded by the *Lovecraft Annual* (item 44).

5. CLARK ASHTON SMITH. *The Black Diamonds*. Edited by S. T. Joshi. 2002 (rpt. 2004). 181 pp.

Notes. Cover and interior illustrations by Jason Eckhardt. First printing, 1040 copies: Morris Publishing.

A transcript of Smith's juvenile novel, probably written at the age of 14 (i.e., c. 1907). The ms. consists of nearly 246 pp. of foolscap sheets that had been sent to the John Hay Library of Brown University in 1979–80 by Smith's literary executor as part of the Clark Ashton Smith Papers there. Joshi began transcribing the text at that time but did not finish until years later. The ms. is missing two sheets; shortly after publication, Dr. W. C. Farmer (see item 17) located them in his effects, and they were made available for transcription. The new printing (184 pp.) incorporates the missing text.

6. A. MERRITT. *The Metal Monster*. Edited by Stefan Dziemianowicz. 2002. 237 pp.

Notes. Cover illustration by Virgil Finlay. First printing, 1050 copies: Morris Publishing. Ten years later, some copies remain in inventory. The first reprint of the 1920 *Argosy All-Story Weekly* serialization of the novel, one of three different texts of the work that appeared in Merritt's lifetime. This is the first title in the "Lovecraft's Library" series, which reprints texts that Lovecraft read and was influenced by. Lovecraft read the text in 1934, when it was lent to him by R. H. Barlow.

7. S. T. JOSHI. *Lovecraft's Library: A Catalogue*. 2002 175 pp.

Contents. Introduction; Explanatory Notes; Lovecraft's Library [981 titles]; Weird &c. Items in Library of H. P. Lovecraft; INDICES: A. Names; B. Titles; C. Works by Lovecraft; D. Publishers; E. Subjects.

Notes. Cover illustration by Jason C. Eckhardt. Our first POD: Lightning Source. Exhaustive revision of the catalogue first published by Necronomicon Press in 1980, with the addition of 60 more titles and listings of tables of contents of many important volumes, along with other additions to the notes. Since publication, some seventeen more titles have been identified.

8. CLARK ASHTON SMITH. *The Last Oblivion: Best Fantastic Poems of Clark Ashton Smith*. Edited by S. T. Joshi and David E. Schultz. 2002. 194 pp.

Contents. Introduction; A Note on the Text; Acknowledgments; THE HASHISH-EATER; OR, THE APOCALYPSE OF EVIL; I. THE STAR-TREADER: The Star-Treader; Ode to the Abyss; Nirvana; The Song of a Comet;

Notes. Cover and interior illustration by Clark Ashton Smith. First printing, 1650 copies, Vaughan Printing, Nashville TN. The first book to feature color reproductions of artwork by Clark Ashton Smith. A kind of stopgap volume while Smith's *Complete Poetry and Translations* (see items 37 and 50) were being prepared. The basic selection was done by Joshi, with additions by Schultz, who supplied the texts based on his years of work with Smith's poetry mss.

9. R. H. BARLOW. *Eyes of the God: The Weird Fiction and Poetry of R. H. Barlow.* Edited by S. T. Joshi, Douglas A. Anderson, and David E. Schultz. 2002. 210 pp.

Contents. Introduction by S. T. Joshi and Douglas A. Anderson. FICTION: The Slaying of the Monster (with H. P. Lovecraft); Eyes of the God; *Annals of the Jinns:* I. The Black Tower; II. The Shadow from Above; III. The Flagon of Beauty; IV. The Sacred Bird; V. The Tomb of the God; VI. The Flower God; VII. The Little Box; VIII. The Fall of the Three Cities; IX. The Mirror; X. The Theft of the Hsothian Manuscripts; XI. An Episode in the Jungle; The Hoard of the Wizard-Beast (with H. P. Lovecraft); The Battle That Ended the Century (with H. P. Lovecraft); The Fidelity of Ghu; The Inhospitable Tavern; The Misfortunes of Butter-Churning; "Till A' the Seas" (with H. P. Lovecraft); The Temple; The Adventures of Garoth; The Experiment; Collapsing Cosmoses (with H. P. Lovecraft); The Bright Valley; The Priest and the Heretic; The Summons; A Dream; A Memory; Pursuit of the Moth; The Root-Gatherers; A Dim-Remembered Story; The Night Ocean (with H. P. Lovecraft); Origin Undetermined; The Swearing of an Oath; The Questioner; The Artizan's Reward; Return by Sunset. POETRY: I. Poems 1936–1939; [Untitled]; Sonnet V; Sonnet VI; Sonnet VII; Song; [Untitled]; Sonnet; [Untitled]; [Untitled]; R. E. H.; St. John's Churchyard; Dirge for the Artist; Alcestis; N. Y.; [Untitled]; [Untitled]; Altamira; Cycle from a Dead Year; H. P. L.; I. March 1937; II. March 1938; [Untitled]; [Untitled]; H. P. L.; H. P. L.; March; [Untitled]; The Unresisting; Shub-Ad; Who Will Not Know; To Bacchus; [Untitled]; [Untitled]; Winter Mood; Burlesque; Frustration; To a Companion; Dawn Delayed; To a Wayfarer; [Untitled]; Fragments; To Alta, On Her Original American Sonnet; Sonnet; [Untitled]; [Untitled]; Fragments; [Untitled]; [Untitled]; [Untitled]; Quetzalcoatl; Quetzalcoatl; Out of the Dark; Prophecy; A Gull From a Cliff; [Untitled]; [Untitled]; [Untitled]; To Sleep; [Untitled]; Isolde; II. POEMS FOR A COMPETITION (1942): Date Uncertain; Nostalgia; For D.; Lines to Diana; The Gods in the Patio; The School Where Nobody Learns What; For Leon Trotzky and Huitzilopochtli; Sacre du Printemps; In Black and White; Explanation to M.; III. [STATEMENT ABOUT POETRY]; IV. VIEW FROM A HILL (1947):

I. For D.; 1. From This Tree; 2. Air for Variations; 3. New Directions; 4. To a Friend on Sailing; 5. To One Rescued; II. Fresco of Priests and Beans; On a Feather Poncho; The Chichimecs; Stela of a Mayan Penitent; Tepuzteca, Tepehua; The Conquered; III. For Rosalie; blotted a beetle; Table Set for Sea-Slime; IV. Five Years; First Year: Sebastian; Second Year: Dream While Paris Was Threatened; Third Year: About a Mythical Factory-Area; Fourth Year: Letter to My Brother; Fifth Year: Viktoria; V. For E. and For W.; "¿Que Quieres? ¿Mis Costillas?" (For E.); Chili Sin Carne (For W.); VI: View from a Hill; To the Builders of a Dam; View from a Hill; Recantation; On the Lights of San Francisco; A Escoger; In Order to Clarify; We Kept on Reading "Tuesday"; VII: For Barbara Mayer; On Leaving Some Friends at an Early Hour; V. A STONE FOR SISIPHUS (1949): Sonnet to Siva; Anniversary; Invocation; Evening; The Coming Fructification by Night of Our Cyrus; Of the Names of the Zapotec Kings; Framed Portent; Orientation to the West; VI. MISCELLANEOUS POEMS: Mourning Song; Admittance; The City; A Tapestry; Warning to Snake Killers; [Untitled]; Mythological Episode; Rainy-Day Pastime; The Heart; Mozart's G. Minor; [Miscellaneous Lines]; Letter for Last Christmas; [Untitled]; Colors; [Untitled]; [Untitled]; [Untitled]; [Untitled]; Poema de Salida; Intimations of Mortality; Bibliography; Index of Poetry Titles; Index of First Lines.

Notes. Cover illustration by R. Saunders (from the *Californian*, Winter 1936, illustrating "The Night Ocean"). An exhaustive edition of Barlow's extant fiction and poetry, including a number of unpublished items derived from Barlow's papers. The fiction was largely edited by Joshi and Schultz, the poetry by Anderson, who also drafted the bibliography.

10.   H. P. LOVECRAFT. *From the Pest Zone: The New York Stories.* Edited by S. T. Joshi and David E. Schultz. 2003. 150 pp.

Contents. Abbreviations; Introduction; The Shunned House; The Horror at Red Hook; He; In the Vault; Cool Air; APPENDIX: Preface to "The Shunned House" by Frank Belknap Long, Jr.; Little Sketches About Town; Notes; Textual Notes.

Notes. Cover illustration by Sean Madden. Interior photographs by Ron Breznay, Donovan K. Loucks, and Steven Mariconda. An extensively annotated edition of the six stories Lovecraft wrote while in New York (1924–26), analogous to the Joshi-Schultz editions of *The Shadow over Innsmouth* (Necronomicon Press, 1994, 1997) and *The Shadow out of Time* (see item 2).

11. HERBERT GORMAN. *The Place Called Dagon.* 2003 (rpt. 2008). 187 pp.

Contents. Introduction, by Larry Creasy; *The Place Called Dagon* by Herbert Gorman; Afterword: Gorman and Lovecraft, by S. T. Joshi.

Notes. Cover design by Barbara Briggs Silbert; interior illustrations by Allen Koszowski. Reprint edition replaced "merman" stock art with illustration by Allen Koszowski. Part of the Lovecraft's Library series. A reprint of Gorman's chilling horror novel of 1927. The Hippocampus staff fortuitously teamed up with Larry Creasy (proprietor of Charon House), who was planning his own reprint; Creasy contributed an extensive biographical introduction, and Joshi added an afterword discussing the novel's possible influence on Lovecraft.

12. JACK MADISON HARINGA. *Drafts from the Moon Pool: The Influence of A. Merritt on H. P. Lovecraft.* 2003. 24 pp.

Notes. Cover photograph of A. Merritt from the collection of Sam Moskowitz. Printed in a numbered edition of 100 copies, the first thirty of which were included in the 30th Anniversary Mailing of the Esoteric Order of Dagon Amateur Press Association. A sensitive essay on Merritt's influence on Lovecraft. Haringa later became coeditor of *Dead Reckonings* (see items 40ff.).

13. H. P. LOVECRAFT. *Letters to Alfred Galpin.* Edited by S. T. Joshi and David E. Schultz. 2003 (rpt. 2004). 287 pp.

Contents. Introduction; Letters to Alfred Galpin; WORKS OF ALFRED GALPIN: Mystery; Two Loves; Selenaio-Phantasma; Remarks to My Handwriting; Marsh-Mad; The Critic; Stars; Some Tendencies of Modern Poetry; The Spoken Tongue; The World Situation; The United's Policy 1920–1921 (with H. P. Lovecraft); Form in Modern Poetry; Picture of a Modern Mood; Nietzsche as a Practical Prophet; To Sam Loveman; The Vivisector; *Four Translations from* Les Fleurs du mal *by Charles Pierre Baudelaire* (Au Lecteur; L'Ennemi; Remords Posthume; L'Ange Gardien); Scattered Remarks upon the Green Cheese Theory; Department of Public Criticism; Intuition in the Philosophy of Bergson; Ennui; A Critic of Poetry; From the French of Pierre de Ronsard ("Amours"—Livre II.): Aubade; Echoes from Beyond Space; Red; En Route (An American to Paris, 1931): I. New York Harbor; II. On Deck; November; A Partial Bibliography of Alfred Galpin; Index.

Notes. Cover design by Anastasia Damianakos. First edition, first printing issued as POD by Booksurge, taken out of print in 2004 and reissued 2004 as first edition, second printing with Lightning Source, our standard POD printer from then on. Booksurge edition lacked frontispiece (photo of AG). The first of what was planned as a series of volumes presenting unabridged and extensively annotated editions of Lovecraft's letters to important correspondents; in the event, only one other volume was published (see item 25). Nearly 50 pp. of Galpin's writings were included.

14. GEORGE STERLING. *The Thirst of Satan: Poems of Fantasy and Terror.* Edited by S. T. Joshi. 215 pp.

Contents. Introduction, by S. T. Joshi; I. THE TESTIMONY OF THE SUNS: The Testimony of the Suns; Mystery; Three Sonnets on Oblivion; Oblivion; The Dust Dethroned; The Night of Gods; Three Sonnets of the Night Skies (I—Aldebaran at Dusk; II—The Chariots of Dawn; III—The Huntress of Stars); The Evanescent; The Thirst of Satan; The Setting of Antares; Outward; The Face of the Skies; Ephemera; Disillusion; The Meteor; The Last Man. II. THE GARDENS OF THE SEA: The Nile; The Fog Siren; The Sea-Fog; Darkness; "Sad Sea-Horizons"; Sonnets by the Night Sea; The Gardens of the Sea; At the Grand Cañon; The Last of Sunset; Caucasus; The Caravan; III. THE MUSE OF THE IN-COMMUNICABLE: Memory of the Dead; The Altar-Flame; Ultima Thule; The Directory; In Extremis; Romance; A Mood; The Moth of Time; The Muse of the Incommunicable; "Omnia Exeunt in Mysterium": To One Self-Slain; Three Sonnets on Sleep; Illusion; Essential Night; To Life; To Science; Waste; Amber; The Dweller in Darkness; Here and Now; IV. THE BLACK VULTURE: The Black Vulture; The Sibyl of Dreams; The Last Monster; "That Walk in Darkness"; To the Mummy of the Lady Isis; Witch-Fire; Song; The Young Witch; Eidolon; The Sphinx; V. THE NAIAD'S SONG: The Haunting; The Naiad's Song; White Magic; The Golden Past; The Revenge; To a Girl Dancing; Flame; The Stranger; VI. A WINE OF WIZARDRY: The Summer of the Gods; Nightmare; A Wine of Wizardry; The Apothecary's; Under the Rainbow; The Shadow of Nirvana; The Wiser Prophet; The Oldest Book; Farm of Fools; VII. THE PASSING OF BIERCE: To Edgar Allan Poe; To Ambrose Bierce; The Ashes in the Sea; The Coming Singer; The Passing of Bierce; Shelley at Spezia. VIII. THE RACK: The Lords of Pain; A Dream of Fear; The Rack; Conspiracy; The Hidden Pool; The Death of Circe; To a Monk's Skull; To Pain; Epilogue: My Swan Song; George Sterling: An Appreciation, by Clark Ashton Smith; Commentary; Index of Titles; Index of First Lines.

Notes. Cover and interior illustrations by Virgil Finlay. A sampling of Sterling's weird verse—the first major reprinting of his poetry since

1969 and a foretaste of the forthcoming edition of his complete poetry and verse drama.

15. LORD DUNSANY. *The Pleasures of a Futuroscope.* Edited by S. T. Joshi. 2003 (rpt. 2005 [paper]). 200 pp.

Notes. Cover illustration by Jeff Remmer. Hardcover edition 1000 copies: Covington Group, St. Louis. The first Hippocampus Press hardcover edition, and the first publication of Dunsany's last novel, probably written in 1955 and unearthed by Joe Doyle, archivist at Dunsany Castle. A splendid fantasy/science fiction hybrid about a man who invents a "futuroscope" that allows him to see into the future—where he finds that a nuclear holocaust has reduced humanity to a primitive state.

16. S. T. JOSHI. *Primal Sources: Essays on H. P. Lovecraft.* 2003. 208 pp.

Contents. Introduction; I. LOVECRAFT THE MAN: Lovecraft and the Munsey Magazines; Lovecraft and *Weird Tales*; A Look at Lovecraft's Letters; Lovecraft and the Films of His Day; Lovecraft's Library; II. LOVECRAFT THE WRITER AND THINKER: Autobiography in Lovecraft; "Reality" and Knowledge; *In Defence of Dagon* and Lovecraft's Philosophy; The Rationale of Lovecraft's Pseudonyms; The Dream World and the Real World in Lovecraft; Lovecraft's Alien Civilisations: A Political Interpetation; Topical References in Lovecraft; III. STUDIES ON INDIVIDUAL WORKS: Lovecraft, Regner Lodbrog, and Olaus Wormius; On "Polaris"; What Happens in "Arthur Jermyn"; "The Tree" and Ancient History; The Sources for "From Beyond"; Lovecraft and the *Regnum Congo*; Lovecraft and Dunsany's *Chronicles of Rodriguez*; On "The Descendant"; Some Sources for "The Mound" and *At the Mountains of Madness*; On "The Book"; Lovecraft's Fantastic Poetry.

Notes. Cover illustration by Robert H. Knox. *Primal Sources* bears the distinction of having been S. T. Joshi's 100th published book. A generous sampling of Joshi's critical essays on Lovecraft, most of them published in *Lovecraft Studies* and *Crypt of Cthulhu* from 1979 onward.

17. CLARK ASHTON SMITH. *The Sword of Zagan and Other Writings.* Edited by Dr. W. C. Farmer. 2004. 181 pp.

Contents. Introduction, by S. T. Joshi; *The Sword of Zagan*; POEMS: The River of Life; The World; The Departed City; Bedouin Song; Zuleika: An Oriental Song; Benares; Rubaiyat of Saiyed; The Isle of Saturn; Temporality; Shapes in the Sunset; Epitaph for the Earth; Night; Rêve Parisien; Averoigne; SHORT STORIES: The Emir's Captive; Fakhreddin; Prince Alcorez and the Magician; The Haunted Gong; The Malay

Creese; The Shah's Messenger; The Bronze Image; The Fulfilled Prophecy; The Haunted Chamber; FRAGMENTS: When the Earth Trembled; Oriental Tales: The Yogi's Ring; The Opal of Delhi [I]; The Opal of Delhi [II]; The Guardian of the Temple; The Emerald Eye; [Untitled]; [Fragment of an essay]; [Letter to Munsey's]; Lost Pages from *The Black Diamonds*; Clark Ashton Smith: A Memoir, by W. C. Farmer.

Notes. Cover and interior illustrations by Jason C. Eckhardt. A follow-up to *The Black Diamonds* (item 5), printing another previously unpublished juvenile novel along with other early stories and fragments. All these items are in the collection of Dr. Farmer, who knew Smith in the latter's final years and was given these mss. over the course of years.

18.   H. P. LOVECRAFT. *Collected Essays, Volume 1: Amateur Journalism.* Edited by S. T. Joshi. 2004. 440 pp.

Contents. Introduction by S. T. Joshi; A Task for Amateur Journalists; Department of Public Criticism (November 1914); Department of Public Criticism (January 1915); Department of Public Criticism (March 1915); What Is Amateur Journalism?; Consolidation's Autopsy; The Amateur Press; Editorial (April 1915); The Question of the Day; The Morris Faction; For President—Leo Fritter; Introducing Mr. Chester Pierce Munroe; [Untitled Notes on Amateur Journalism]; Department of Public Criticism (May 1915); Finale; New Department Proposed: Instruction for the Recruit; Our Candidate; Exchanges; For Historian— Ira A. Cole; Editorial (July 1915); The Conservative and His Critics (July 1915); Some Political Phases; Introducing Mr. John Russell; In a Major Key; Amateur Notes; The Dignity of Journalism; Department of Public Criticism (September 1915); Editorial (October 1915); The Conservative and His Critics (October 1915); The Youth of Today; An Impartial Spectator; [Untitled Notes on Amateur Journalism]; Little Journeys to the Homes of Prominent Amateurs: II. Andrew Francis Lockhart; Report of First Vice-President (November 1915); Department of Public Criticism (December 1915); Systematic Instruction in the United; United Amateur Press Association: Exponent of Amateur Journalism; Introducing Mr. James Pyke; Report of First Vice-President (January 1916); Editorial (February 1916); Department of Public Criticism (April 1916); Among the New-Comers; Department of Public Criticism (June 1916); Department of Public Criticism (August 1916); Department of Public Criticism (September 1916); Among the Amateurs; Concerning "Persia—in Europe"; Amateur Standards; A Request; Department of Public Criticism (March 1917); Department of Public Criticism (May 1917); A Reply to *The Lingerer*; The United's Problem; Editorially; The "Other United"; Department of Public Criticism (July

1917); Little Journeys to the Homes of Prominent Amateurs: V. Eleanor J. Barnhart; News Notes (July 1917); President's Message (September 1917); President's Message (November 1917); President's Message (January 1918); Department of Public Criticism (January 1918); President's Message (March 1918); Department of Public Criticism (March 1918); President's Message (May 1918); Department of Public Criticism (May 1918); Comment; President's Message (July 1918); Amateur Criticism; The United 1917–1918; The Amateur Press Club; *Les Mouches Fantastiques*; Department of Public Criticism (September 1918); Department of Public Criticism (November 1918); News Notes (November 1918); [Letter to the Bureau of Critics]; Department of Public Criticism (January 1919); Department of Public Criticism (March 1919); Winifred Virginia Jordan: Associate Editor; Helene Hoffman Cole—Litterateur; Department of Public Criticism (May 1919); Trimmings; For Official Editor—Anne Tillery Renshaw; Amateurdom; Looking Backward; For What Does the United Stand?; The Pseudo-United; The Conquest of the Hub Club; News Notes (September 1920); Amateur Journalism: Its Possible Needs and Betterment; Editorial (November 1920); News Notes (November 1920); News Notes (January 1921); The United's Policy 1920–1921 (with Alfred Galpin); What Amateurdom and I Have Done for Each Other; News Notes (March 1921); The Vivisector (March 1921); [Letter to John Milton Heins]; Lucubrations Lovecraftian; News Notes (May 1921); The Vivisector (June 1921); The Haverhill Convention; News Notes (July 1921); Within the Gates; The Convention Banquet; Editorial (September 1921); News Notes (September 1921); A Singer of Ethereal Moods and Fancies; News Notes (November 1921); [Letter to John Milton Heins]; Editorial (January 1922); News Notes (January 1922); *Rainbow* Called Best First Issue; News Notes (March 1922); The Vivisector (March 1922); News Notes (May 1922); [Letter to the N.A.P.A.]; President's Message (November 1922–January 1923); President's Message (March 1923); Bureau of Critics (March 1923); Rursus Adsumus; The Vivisector (Spring 1923); President's Message (May 1923); Lovecraft's Greeting; President's Message (July 1923); [Untitled Notes on Amateur Journalism]; The President's Annual Report; Trends and Objects; Editorial (May 1924); News Notes (May 1924); Editorial (July 1925); News Notes (July 1925); A Matter of Uniteds; The Convention; Bureau of Critics (December 1931); Critics Submit First Report; Verse Criticism; Report of Bureau of Critics; Bureau of Critics Comment on Verse, Typography, Prose; Bureau of Critics (June 1934); Chairman of the Bureau of Critics Reports on Poetry; Mrs. Miniter—Estimates and Recollections; Report of the Bureau of Critics (December 1934); Report of the Bureau of Critics (March 1935); Lovecraft Offers Verse Criticism;

Dr. Eugene B. Kuntz; Some Current Amateur Verse; Report of the Executive Judges; Some Current Motives and Practices; [Letter to the N.A.P.A.]; [Literary Review]; Defining the "Ideal" Paper; APPENDIX: [Miscellaneous Notes in the *United Amateur*]; Official Organ Fund; [Untitled Note on Amateur Poetry]; [On *Notes High and Low* by Carrie Adams Berry]; [A Voice from the Grave]; Index.

Notes. Cover illustration (uniform for all five volumes of the series) by Virgil Finlay. Published simultaneously in hardcover and paperback. Hardcover 250 copies, Covington Group. One of the most ambitious projects undertaken by Hippocampus Press—the publication of Lovecraft's complete nonfiction writings, arranged thematically, with extensive annotations. Previously these writings had been scattered throughout many Arkham House volumes, including Joshi's edition of *Miscellaneous Writings* (Arkham House, 1995); but many items remained unreprinted.

19.   H. P. LOVECRAFT. *Collected Essays, Volume 2: Literary Criticism.* Edited by S. T. Joshi. 2004. 248 pp.

Contents. Introduction, by S. T. Joshi; Metrical Regularity; The Allowable Rhyme; The Proposed Authors' Union; The Vers Libre Epidemic; Poesy; The Despised Pastoral; The Literature of Rome; The Simple Spelling Mania; The Case for Classicism; Literary Composition; Editor's Note to "A Scene for *Macbeth*" by Samuel Loveman; Winifred Virginia Jackson: A "Different" Poetess; The Poetry of Lilian Middleton; Lord Dunsany and His Work; Rudis Indigestaque Moles; Introduction [to *The Poetical Works of Jonathan E. Hoag*]; Ars Gratia Artis; In the Editor's Study; [Random Notes]; [Review of *Ebony and Crystal* by Clark Ashton Smith]; The Professional Incubus; The Omnipresent Philistine; The Work of Frank Belknap Long, Jr.; Supernatural Horror in Literature; Preface [to *White Fire* by John Ravenor Bullen]; Notes on "Alias Peter Marchall", by A. F. Lorenz; Foreword [to *Thoughts and Pictures* by Eugene B. Kuntz]; Notes on Verse Technique; Weird Story Plots; [Notes on Weird Fiction]; Notes on Writing Weird Fiction; Some Notes on Interplanetary Fiction; What Belongs in Verse; [Suggestions for a Reading Guide]; APPENDIX: The Poetry of John Ravenor Bullen; The Favourite Weird Stories of H. P. Lovecraft; Supernatural Horror in Literature; Index.

Notes. Cover illustration by Virgil Finlay. Simultaneously published in hardcover and paperback. Hardcover 250 copies, Covington Group. The slimmest of the five volumes of *Collected Essays.*

20. S. T. JOSHI AND DAVID E. SCHULTZ. *An H. P. Lovecraft Encyclopedia.* 2004. xx, 339 pp.

Notes. Cover design by Gaile Ivaska. Paperback reprint of the edition first published by Greenwood Press (2001), with a few additions and corrections.

21. ALGERNON BLACKWOOD. *Incredible Adventures.* 2004. 224 pp.

Contents. Introduction by S. T. Joshi; The Regeneration of Lord Ernie; The Sacrifice; The Damned; A Descent into Egypt; Wayfarers.

Notes. Cover illustration by W. Graham Robertson (from the 1916 Macmillan edition of Blackwood's *The Centaur*). Part of the Lovecraft's Library series. A reprint of Blackwood's classic story collection of 1914, which Joshi regards as one of the greatest weird volumes of all time.

22. S. T. JOSHI. *The Evolution of the Weird Tale.* 2004. 216 pp.

Contents. Introduction; I. SOME AMERICANS OF THE GOLDEN AGE: W. C. Morrow: Horror in San Francisco; Robert W. Chambers: The Bohemian Weird Tale; F. Marion Crawford: Blood-and-Thunder Horror; Edward Lucas White: Dream and Reality; II. SOME ENGLISH-MEN OF THE GOLDEN AGE: Sir Arthur Quiller-Couch: Ghosts and Scholars; Rudyard Kipling: The Horror of India; E. F. Benson: Spooks and More Spooks; L. P. Hartley: The Refined Ghost; III. H. P. LOVE-CRAFT AND HIS INFLUENCE: H. P. Lovecraft: The Fiction of Materialism; Frank Belknap Long: Things from the Sea; A Literary Tutelage: Robert Bloch and H. P. Lovecraft; Passing the Torch: H. P. Lovecraft and Fritz Leiber; IV. CONTEMPORARIES: Rod Serling: The Moral Supernatural; L. P. Davies: The Workings of the Mind; Les Daniels: The Horror of History; Dennis Etchison: Spanning the Genres; David J. Schow and Splatterpunk; Poppy Z. Brite: Sex, Horror, and Rock-&-Roll; Bibliography.

Notes. Cover illustration by Wallace Smith (from Ben Hecht's *Fantazius Mallare*, 1922). A loose follow-up of Joshi's previous treatises, *The Weird Tale* (Univ. of Texas Press, 1990) and *The Modern Weird Tale* (McFarland, 2001), covering authors from the mid-19th century to the present day, including three chapters (on Les Daniels, Dennis Etchison, and David J. Schow) that had been scheduled to appear in *The Modern Weird Tale* but were omitted for space reasons.

23. SAMUEL LOVEMAN. *Out of the Immortal Night: Selected Works of Samuel Loveman.* Edited by S. T. Joshi and David E. Schultz. 2004. 244 pp.

Contents. Introduction, by S. T. Joshi; I. POETRY: *Poems* (1911): In Pierrot's Garden; Ode to Ceres; Fra Angelico; Song; To P. G.; Lines; A Twenty-second Birthday; *The Hermaphrodite and Other Poems* (1936): The Hermaphrodite; River Pattern; Will o' the Wisp; Steener Haakonson Dances; Dream Song; Heckscher Building; Euphorion; Agathon; Arcesilaus; Lineage; For a Book of Poems; Ascension; Thomas Holley Chivers; The Ramapos; Oscar Wilde; John Clare in a Madhouse; The Minstrel; The Chopin-Player; A Dedication; Vice; Transience; Dolore; Bacchanale; To Simone's; Ad Fratrem; Isolation; Remonstrance; Proteus; A Voyage; Legend; The Return; Memoralia; Forest of Rhododendron; Understanding; Ecce Homo; Ariel; Visitor; Inarticulate; Madison Square; Contrast; Invocation; Song; Harbour; Admonition; Foes; Limbo; Interlude; Gates Mills; Wasteland; Amy Levy; Forest Hill; Andenkung; Dream of Spring; Finis; A Georgia Garden; Palingenesis; Belated Love; Nostalgia; Becalmed; Mutation; Dirge; To Dionysus; To Apollo; Quatrains (Poppies; Forgotten Poets; Space; Music; Simeon Solomon; Aftermath); A Chinese Pavilion; Ben De Casseres in Camden; Terminus; UNCOLLECTED POEMS: A Poet; A Sonnet: Lethe; The Birth of Fear; Pierced; A Lily; Lost Youth; Avalon; Hope; The Old Cobbler; Shadow-Land; The Song Unsung; Ship of Dreams; The Birth of Poesy; On Lost Friendship; Peccavi; The Plaint of Bygone Loves; Eventide (I. Sunset; II. Twilight; III. Night); David Gray; An Epitaph; Quatrains; To Alfred Noyes, Oversea; Michael Scott's Wooing; Thomas Dermody; Resurgam; Shadow-Love; Euthanasia; A Burden; A Song of Chamisso's; A Departure; W. E.; On the Passing of Youth; A Triumph in Eternity; Talent; [Untitled]; Adventure; In Sepulcretis; Saturday Evening; A Letter to G—— K——; Ernest Nelson; Heldenleben; Winter; To Satan; Christmas—1923; Genesis; Night Piece (Forest Hill); Monolith; Oscar Redivivus; Unfulfilled; To Mr. Theobald; To George Kirk on His 27th Birthday; Music; Vigil; To a Child; The Dead King; Kin; Episode; Rescue; Transit; An Admonition to the Ladies; Debs in Prison; For the Chelsea Book Shop [I]; For the Chelsea Book Shop [II]; Nepenthe; Quatrain; Reliquiae; Spring at El Retiro; Versailles; [Untitled]; The Goal; John Clare in 1864; II. DRAMA: Oedipus at Colonus; Belshazzar; Nero; Narcisse; Arcady; A Scene for *King Lear*; A Scene for *Macbeth*; The Sphinx: A Conversation; III. TRANSLATIONS: Twenty-four Translations from Heine; Catullus; Translations from Baudelaire: La Musique; Parfum Exotique; Horreur Sympathique; De Profundis Clamavi; La Beauté; Causerie; Chant d'Automne; Le Couvercle; Le Chat; La Fontaine de Sang; Sonnet d'Automne; Ciel

Brouillé; Les Chats; Translations from Verlaine: Sagesse; Bruxelles; Romances sans Paroles; Il Bacio; La Bonne Chanson; Vert; Sappho; Sonnet: After Leconte de Lisle; God's Work; IV. FICTION: Antenor; The Faun; The Dog; An Impression; The One Who Found Pity; Christmas-Eve with Sherlock Holmes; V. ESSAYS: Mr. Sterling and Minor Poets; A Keats Discovery; Modern Poetry (An Exorcism); A Note [to *Twenty-one Letters of Ambrose Bierce*]; A Convention Address; The Book of Life; Foreword to *Poppies and Mandragora*; Preface to *The Man from Genoa*; Hubert Crackanthorpe: A Realist of the Nineties; Marcel Proust; Literature and Dry-rot; A Letter on Hart Crane; Howard Phillips Lovecraft; Lovecraft as Conversationalist; Bibliography; Index of Poetry Titles; Index of First Lines.

Notes. Cover illustration by William Sommer (from the 1944 W. Paul Cook edition of Loveman's *The Sphinx*). The product of many years' work by the editors in gathering Loveman's writings (chiefly his poetry) from amateur journals and unpublished manuscripts. All Loveman's known poetry was included, but only selections of his essays, reviews, and amateur journalism.

24. R. NEMO HILL. *The Strange Music of Erich Zann.* 2004. 51 pp.

Notes. Cover illustration by Joe Werhle, Jr. With audio CD of the author reading his work. Booklet was issued in late 2004, but the CD was not produced until early the following year, hence it bears a 2005 copyright date. A long poem based on H. P. Lovecraft's tale "The Music of Erich Zann" (1921).

25. H. P. LOVECRAFT. *Letters to Rheinhart Kleiner.* Edited by S. T. Joshi and David E. Schultz. 2005. 298 pp.

Contents. Introduction; Letters to Rheinhart Kleiner; WORKS: A. POEMS BY RHEINHART KLEINER: Alas!; Dream Days, or, Metrical Musings; Another Endless Day; Motes; At Providence in 1918; Brooklyn, My Brooklyn; Epistle to Mr. and Mrs. Lovecraft; The Four of Us!; After a Decade; H. P. L.; B. ESSAYS BY RHEINHART KLEINER: A Note on Howard P. Lovecraft's Verse; The Kleicomolo; After a Decade and the Kalem Club; Howard Phillips Lovecraft; Lovecraft in Brooklyn; Some Lovecraft Memories; C. RHEINHART KLEINER VS. H. P. LOVECRAFT: To Mary of the Movies [Kleiner]; To Charlie of the Comics [Lovecraft]; To a Movie Star [Kleiner]; To Mistress Sophia Simple, Queen of the Cinema [Lovecraft]; Ruth [Kleiner]; Grace [Lovecraft]; John Oldham: 1653–1683 [Kleiner]; John Oldham: A Defence [Lovecraft]; Ethel: Cashier in a Broad Street Buffet [Kleiner]; Cindy: Scrub-Lady in a State Street Skyscraper [Lovecraft]; On Collaboration; D. POEMS BY H. P.

LOVECRAFT ADDRESSED TO RHEINHART KLEINER: The Bookstall; Content; To Mr. Kleiner, on Receiving from Him the Poetical Works of Addison, Gay, and Somerville; R. Kleiner, Laureatus, in Heliconem; To Rheinhart Kleiner, Esq., Upon His Town Fables and Elegies; [On Rheinhart Kleiner Being Hit by an Automobile]; A Partial Bibliography of Rheinhart Kleiner; Index.

Notes. Cover design by Anastasia Damianakos (uniform with item 13). Complete publication of Lovecraft's letters to Kleiner, including lengthy letters to the Kleicomolo correspondence circle. Includes a generous selection of Kleiner's writings, including his poetry and essays, as well as poems by Lovecraft addressed to Kleiner.

26.   M. P. SHIEL. *The House of Sounds and Others.* Edited by S. T. Joshi. 2005. 299 pp.

Contents. Introduction, by S. T. Joshi; Xélucha; The Pale Ape; The Case of Euphemia Raphash; Huguenin's Wife; The House of Sounds; The Great King; The Bride; *The Purple Cloud*; APPENDIX: Vaila.

Notes. Cover illustration by J. T. Lindroos. A small number of copies were printed bearing an erroneous price ($15.00 instead of $20.00). Some made their way into circulation before the error was caught and corrected. Part of the Lovecraft's Library series. An extensive selection of those works by Shiel that Lovecraft read and might have been influenced by, including the 1901 edition of *The Purple Cloud* (substantially different from the revised edition of 1929).

27.   ROBERT M. PRICE, EDITOR. *Tales out of Dunwich.* 2005. 302 pp.

Contents. Dunwich Homecoming, by Robert M. Price; *The Thing in the Woods*, by Harper Williams; The Mark of the Monster, by Jack Williamson; The Thing from Lover's Lane, by Nancy A. Collins; Acute Spiritual Fear, by Robert M. Price; Black Brat of Dunwich, by Stanley C. Sargent; The Dunwich Lodger, by Brian McNaughton; The Doom That Came to Dunwich, by Richard A. Lupoff; The Dunwich Gate, by Don D'Ammassa; The N-Scale Horror, by Gerard E. Giannattasio; Dunwich Dreams, Dunwich Screams, by Eddy C. Bertin.

Notes. Cover illustration by Philip Fuller. The illustration bears more than a passing resemblance to Anastasia Damianakos. A large anthology featuring tales about Dunwich, including the first reprint of Harper Williams's short novel *The Thing in the Woods* (1924), which clearly influenced some elements of Lovecraft's "The Dunwich Horror" (1928).

28. GEORGE STERLING AND CLARK ASHTON SMITH. *The Shadow of the Unattained: The Letters of George Sterling and Clark Ashton Smith*. Edited by David E. Schultz and S. T. Joshi. 2005. 342 pp.

Contents. Introduction; The Shadow of the Unattained; APPENDIX: To George Sterling, by Clark Ashton Smith; To George Sterling, by Clark Ashton Smith; To George Sterling, by Clark Ashton Smith; To the Editor of *Town Talk*, by Ambrose Bierce; The Coming Singer, by George Sterling; Preface to *Odes and Sonnets*, by George Sterling; Preface to *Ebony and Crystal*, by George Sterling; Recent Books of Fact and Fiction, by George Sterling; Poetry of the Pacific Coast—California, by George Sterling; To George Sterling: A Valediction, by Clark Ashton Smith; George Sterling: An Appreciation, by Clark Ashton Smith; George Sterling: Poet and Friend, by Clark Ashton Smith; To George Sterling, by Clark Ashton Smith; Glossary of Names; List of Extant Enclosures; Bibliography; Index.

Notes. Cover illustration by Philip Fuller (based on a photograph of Sterling and Smith). Fifteen interior illustrations from drawings by Smith from his letters to Sterling. Unabridged and annotated edition of the complete extant correspondence of the two writers, who wrote extensively to each other from 1911 until Sterling's death in 1926. Also included are writings by each author about the other.

29. H. P. LOVECRAFT. *Collected Essays, Volume 3: Science*. Edited by S. T. Joshi. 2005. 357 pp.

Contents. Introduction, by S. T Joshi; My Opinion as to the Lunar Canals; No Transit of Mars; Trans-Neptunian Planets; The Moon; The Earth Not Hollow. ASTRONOMY ARTICLES FOR THE *PAWTUXET VALLEY GLEANER*: The Heavens for August; The Skies of September; Is Mars an Inhabited World?; Is There Life on the Moon?; An Interesting Phenomenon; October Heavens; Are There Undiscovered Planets?; Can the Moon Be Reached by Man?; The Moon; [Untitled]; The Sun; The Leonids; Comets; December Skies; The Fixed Stars; Clusters—Nebulae; January Heavens; ASTRONOMY ARTICLES FOR THE PROVIDENCE *TRIBUNE*: In the August Sky; The September Heavens; Astronomy in October; The Skies of November; The Heavens for December; The Heavens in January; The Heavens in February; The Heavens in March; April Skies; The Heavens in May; The Heavens in June; Astronomy in August; The Heavens for September; The Skies of October; The Heavens in November; Heavens for December; The Heavens in January; February Skies; The Heavens in Month of March; Solar Eclipse Feature of June Heavens; Third Annual Report of the Prov. Meteorological Station; Celestial Objects for All; Venus and the Public Eye; ASTRONOMY ARTICLES FOR THE PROVIDENCE *EVENING NEWS:* The January Sky; The February Sky; The March Sky; The April Sky; May Sky; The June Sky; The July Sky; The August Sky; The September Sky; The October Sky; The November Sky; The December Sky; The January Sky; The February Sky; The March Sky; April Skies; The May Sky; The June Skies; The July Skies; The August Skies; September Skies; October Skies; November Skies; December Skies; January Skies; February Skies; March Skies; April Skies; May Skies; June Skies; July Skies; August Skies; September Skies; October Skies; November Skies; December Skies; January Skies; February Skies; March Skies; April Skies; May Skies; June Skies; July Skies; August Skies; September Skies; October Skies; November Skies; December Skies; January Skies; February Skies; March Skies; April Skies; May Skies; SCIENCE VERSUS CHARLATANRY: Science versus Charlatanry; The Falsity of Astrology; Astrology and the Future; Delavan's Comet and Astrology; The Fall of Astrology; [Isaac Bickerstaffe's Reply]; MYSTERIES OF THE HEAVENS REVEALED BY ASTRONOMY: I. The Sky and Its Contents; [II.] The Solar System; III. The Sun; IV. The Inferior Planets; V. Eclipses; VI. The Earth and Its Moon; VII. Mars and the Asteroids; VIII. The Outer Planets; [The Outer Planets, Part II]; IX. Comets and Meteors; Comets and Meteors [Part II]; X. The Stars; [The Stars, Part II]; XI. Clusters and Nebulae; [Clusters and Nebulae, Part II]; XII. The Constellations; [The Constellations, Part II]; XIII. Telescopes and Observatories; [Telescopes and Observatories, Part II]; Editor's Note to "The Irish and the Fairies" by Peter J. MacManus; Brumalia; The Truth about Mars; The Cancer of Superstition; [Some Backgrounds of Fairyland]; APPENDIX: Does "Vulcan" Exist?; Astronomical Notebook; [Astrology Articles by J. F. Hartmann]: Astrology and the European War; [Letter to the Editor]; The Science of Astrology; A Defense of Astrology; Lovecraft's Juvenile Scientific Manuscripts; Index.

Notes. Cover illustration by Virgil Finlay. Interior illustrations by Lovecraft. Hardcover 250 copies, Covington Group. Simultaneously published in hardcover and paperback. Complete publication of Lovecraft's scientific writings, including the first unabridged reprint of his dozens of astronomy columns for Providence newspapers (1906–18).

30.   H. P. LOVECRAFT. *Collected Essays, Volume 4: Travel.* Edited by S. T. Joshi. 2005. 300 pp.

Contents. Introduction, by S. T. Joshi; The Trip of Theobald; Vermont—A First Impression; Observations on Several Parts of America; Travels in the Provinces of America; An Account of a Trip to the Antient Fairbanks House, in Dedham, and to the Red Horse Tavern in Sudbury, in the Province of the Massachusetts-Bay; Account of a Visit to Charleston, S.C.; An Account of *Charleston*, in His Maj^{ty's} Province of *South-Carolina*; A Description of the Town of Quebeck in New-France, Lately Added to His Britannick Majesty's Dominions; European Glimpses; Some Dutch Footprints in New England; Homes and Shrines of Poe; The Unknown City in the Ocean; Charleston; APPENDIX: A Descent to Avernus; Sleepy Hollow To-day; Index.

Notes. Cover illustration by Virgil Finlay, interior illustrations by Lovecraft. Hardcover 250 copies, Covington Group. Simultaneously published in hardcover and paperback. First complete edition of Lovecraft's travel writings, including the first publication of two brief travelogues.

31.   ROBERT H. WAUGH. *The Monster in the Mirror: Looking for H. P. Lovecraft.* 2006. 302 pp.

Contents. Introduction; PART I: FIRST PRINCIPLES: Lovecraft's Hands; Documents, Creatures, and History; PART II: SORTIES: "The Picture in the House": Images of Complicity; *At the Mountains of Madness:* The Subway and the Shoggoth; PART III: MEDITATIONS ON "THE OUTSIDER": "The Outsider," the Terminal Climax, and Other Conclusions; Lovecraft and Keats Confront the "Awful Rainbow"; The Outsider, the Autodidact, and Other Professions; PART IV: MATERIALISM, THEOLOGY, AND IMAGINATION: Lovecraft and Leopardi: Sunsets and Moonsets; Lovecraft Born Again: An Essay in Apologetic Criticism; Works Cited; Index.

Notes. Cover illustration by Philip Fuller. An extensive selection of Waugh's critical essays on Lovecraft, most of them published in *Lovecraft Studies.*

32.   MARA KIRK HART AND S. T. JOSHI, EDITORS. *Lovecraft's New York Circle: The Kalem Club, 1924–1927.* 2006. 240 pp.

Contents. Preface, by Peter Cannon; Introduction, by Mara Kirk Hart; THE KALEM LETTERS OF GEORGE KIRK: Introduction, by Mara Kirk Hart; 1924; 1925; 1926; 1927; WRITINGS BY THE KALEMS: GEORGE KIRK: Book Collecting: The Prince of Hobbies; RHEINHART KLEINER: A Glee; At Providence in 1918; Epistle to Mr. and Mrs. Lovecraft; The Four of Us (Rondeau); Brooklyn, My Brooklyn; Columbia Heights, Brooklyn; [Prisky]; On a Favorite Cat: Killed by an Automobile; To George W. Kirk, Upon His 26th Birthday; To His Peculiar Friend, G. Kirk, Esq.; Your Street; Blue Pencil Anniversary Song; What My Ancestors Were Like; The Great Adventure; If I Had Lived a Hundred

Years Ago; H. P. L.; ARTHUR LEEDS: He Had to Pay the Nine-Tailed Cat; FRANK BELKNAP LONG: A Man from Genoa; Come, Let Us Make; The Man Who Died Twice; H. P. LOVECRAFT: Plaster-All; To Endymion; Providence; Waste Paper; Primavera; To an Infant; To George Kirk, Esq.; To George Willard Kirk, Gent., of Chelsea Village in New York, upon His Birthday, Novr. 25, 1925; Two Christmas Poems to G. W. K.; A Year Off; In Memoriam Oscar Incoul Verelst of Manhattan 1920–1926; SAMUEL LOVEMAN: A Letter to G—— K——; To George Kirk on His 27th Birthday; For the Chelsea Book Shop [1]; For the Chelsea Book Shop [2]; For a Cat; For a Book of Poems; Admonition; Limbo; To H. P. L.; Genesis; Spring at El Retiro; Arcesilaus; John Clare in 1864; EVERETT MCNEIL: From *Tonty of the Iron Hand*; JAMES FERDINAND MORTON: To G.W.K. on His 27th Birthday; From *The Curse of Race Prejudice*; APPENDIX: After a Decade and the Kalem Club, by Rheinhart Kleiner; Bards and Bibliophiles, by Rheinhart Kleiner; Sources and Works Consulted; Index.

Notes. Cover illustration by Barbara Briggs Silbert. An innovative volume conceived and largely executed by Mara Kirk Hart (daughter of George Kirk), in which selections of the writings by the major members of the Kalem Club (George Kirk, Rheinhart Kleiner, Arthur Leeds, Frank Belknap Long, H. P. Lovecraft, Samuel Loveman, Everett McNeil, and James Ferdinand Morton) are reprinted; a few items are previously unpublished. The selections are preceded by an invaluable selection of letters written by Kirk to his fiancée, Lucile Dvorak (1924–27), shedding much light on the Kalems' activities in New York during and just after the period of Lovecraft's residence there.

33. SCOTT CONNORS, EDITOR. *The Freedom of Fantastic Things: Selected Criticism on Clark Ashton Smith.* 2006. 376 pp.

Contents. Introduction, by Scott Connors; The Centaur, by Clark Ashton Smith; Klarkash-Ton and "Greek," by Donald Sidney-Fryer; Contemporary Reviews of Clark Ashton Smith; Eblis in Bakelite, by James Blish; James Blish versus Clark Ashton Smith, to Wit, the Young Turk Syndrome, by Donald Sidney-Fryer; The Last Romantic, by S. J. Sackett; Communicable Mysteries: The Last True Symbolist, by Fred Chappell; What Happens in *The Hashish-Eater?*, by S. T. Joshi; The Babel of Visions: The Structuration of Clark Ashton Smith's *The Hashish-Eater*, by Dan Clore; Clark Ashton Smith's "Nero," by Carl Jay Buchanan; Satan Speaks: A Reading of "Satan Unrepentant," by Phillip A. Ellis; Lands Forgotten or Unfound: The Prose Poetry of Clark Ashton Smith, by S. T. Joshi; Outside the Human Aquarium: The Fantastic Imagination of Clark Ashton Smith, by Brian Stableford; Clark Ashton

Smith: Master of the Macabre; John Kipling Hitz; Gesturing Toward the Infinite: Clark Ashton Smith and Modernism, by Scott Connors; Clark Ashton Smith: A Note on the Aesthetics of Fantasy, by Charles K. Wolfe; Fantasy and Decadence in the Work of Clark Ashton Smith, by Lauric Guillaud; Humor in Hyperspace: Smith's Uses of Satire, by John Kipling Hitz; Song of the Necromancer: "Loss" in Clark Ashton Smith's Fiction, by Steve Behrends; Brave World Old and New: The Atlantis Theme in the Poetry and Fiction of Clark Ashton Smith, by Donald Sidney-Fryer; Coming In from the Cold: Incursions of "Outsideness" in Hyperborea, by Steven Tompkins; As Shadows Wait upon the Sun: Clark Ashton Smith's Zothique, by Jim Rockhill; Into the Woods: The Human Geography of Averoigne, by Stefan Dziemianowicz; Sorcerous Style: Clark Ashton Smith's *The Double Shadow and Other Fantasies*, by Peter H. Goodrich; Loss and Recuperation: A Model for Reading Clark Ashton Smith's "Xeethra," by Dan Clore; "Life, Love, and the Clemency of Death": A Reexamination of Clark Ashton Smith's "The Isle of the Torturers," by Scott Connors; Regarding the Providence Point of View, by Ronald S. Hilger; An Annotated Chronology of the Fiction of Clark Ashton Smith, by Steve Behrends; Bibliography; Contributors; Acknowledgments; Index.

Notes. Cover illustration by Frank Kupka ("Resistance, or the Black Idol," 1903). Simultaneously published in hardcover and paperback. The most extensive selection ever published of criticism of Clark Ashton Smith, including both reprinted and previously unpublished essays.

34.   BENJAMIN SZUMSKYJ, EDITOR. *Two-Gun Bob: A Centennial Study of Robert E. Howard.* 2006. 233 pp.

Contents. Robert E. Howard: A Texan Master, by Michael Moorcock; Robert E. Howard: A Look at "Two-Gun Bob" 100 Years On, by Benjamin Szumskyj; *The Junto*: Being a Brief Look at the Amateur Press Association Robert E. Howard Partook In as a Youth, by Glenn Lord; . . . From Acorns Grow: Robert E. Howard Revealed in *Post Oaks and Sand Roughs*, by John Goodrich; Sleuths, Secrets, and Grisly Mysteries: The Detective Fiction of Robert E. Howard, by Fred Blosser; Words from the Outer Dark: The Poetical Works of Robert E. Howard, by Michele Tetro; Texas Talespinner: Robert E. Howard's Ways with Words, by Frank Coffman; Robert E. Howard: A Behavioral Perspective, by Charles Gramlich, Ph.D.; The Persistence of the Familiar: The Hyborian World and the Geographies of Fantastic Literature, by Lorenzo Di-Tommaso, Ph.D.; Bran Mak Morn and History, by S. T. Joshi; "Bitter Pleasures and Swinish Stupidity": Howard's Take on Human Character, by Charles Hoffman; El Borak, the Swift, by Scott Sheaffer; Stars and Strong Men: The Science and Cosmic Fiction of Robert E. Howard, by Martin Andersson; Laudator Temporis Acti: History and Myth in the Works of Robert E. Howard, by Pietro Guarriello; Cimmerian Gloves: Studying Robert E. Howard's Ace Jessel from the Ringside, by Benjamin Szumskyj; About the Contributors; Acknowledgments; Index.

Notes. Cover illustration by Frank Coffman. A generous sampling of criticism of Howard to commemorate the centennial of his birth.

35.   W. H. PUGMIRE. *The Fungal Stain and Other Dreams.* 2006. 179 pp.

Contents. An Eidolon of Nothing; Hour of Their Appetite; The Sign That Sets the Darkness Free; Jigsaw Boy; The Fungal Stain; Balm of Nepenthe; Some Darker Star; The Saprophytic Fungi; A Phantom of Beguilement; Stupor Mundi; Past the Gate of Deepest Slumber; His Splintered Kiss; Oh, Baleful Theophany; The Strange Dark Folk; Your Metamorphic Moan.

Notes. Cover illustration and interior illustrations by Robert H. Knox. A volume of Pugmire's recent weird writings, many of them in the Lovecraftian vein. The first Hippocampus Press publication of original fiction by a contemporary writer.

36.   H. P. LOVECRAFT. *Collected Essays, Volume 5: Philosophy; Autobiography and Miscellany.* Edited by S. T. Joshi. 2006. 382 pp.

Contents. Introduction, by S. T. Joshi; PHILOSOPHY: The Crime of the Century; The Renaissance of Manhood; Liquor and Its Friends; More *Chain Lightning*; Symphony and Stress; Old England and the "Hyphen"; Revolutionary Mythology; The Symphonic Ideal; "Editor's Note" to "The Genesis of the Revolutionary War" by Henry Clapham McGavack; A Remarkable Document; At the Root; Time and Space; Merlinus Redivivus; Anglo-Saxondom; Amer-icanism; The League; Bolshevism; Idealism and Materialism—A Reflection; Life for Humanity's Sake; [*In Defence of Dagon*]; Nietzscheism and Realism; East and West Harvard Conservatism; The Materialist Today; Some Causes of Self-Immolation; Some Repetitions on the Times; A Layman Looks at the Government; The *Journal* and the New Deal; A Living Heritage: Roman Architecture in Today's America; Objections to Orthodox Communism; AUTOBIOGRAPHY AND MISCELLANY: The Brief Autobiography of an Inconsequential Scribbler; A Confession of Unfaith; [Diary: 1925]; [Commercial Blurbs]; Cats and Dogs; Notes on Hudson Valley History; Autobiography of Howard Phillips Lovecraft; In Memoriam: Henry St. Clair Whitehead; Some Notes on a Nonentity;

Correspondence between R. H. Barlow and Wilson Shepherd of Oakman, Alabama—Sept.–Nov. 1932; In Memoriam: Robert Ervin Howard; Commonplace Book; Instructions in Case of Decease; [Diary—1937]; NOTES FOR STORIES: [Notes to "Medusa's Coil"]; [Notes to *At the Mountains of Madness*]; [Notes to "The Shadow over Innsmouth"]; [The Round Tower]; [The Rose Window]; Of Evil Sorceries Done in New-England, of Daemons in No Humane Shape; [Notes to "The Shadow out of Time"]; [Notes to "The Challenge From Beyond"]; MISCELLANEOUS LISTS AND NOTES; [1] Catalogue of Prov. Press Co.; [2] [Catalogue of Works (1902)]; [3] [Postal Expenses]; [4] Old Farmer's Almanacks Wanted by H. P. Lovecraft; [5] [Notes on Clothing Stores]; [6] [Works Desired by H. Warner Munn]; [7] [Works of Weird Fiction]; [8] Tales by H. P. Lovecraft; [9] Basic Books for a Weird Library; [10] [Remembrancer]; [11] [List of Amateur Papers]; [12] [Possible Collections of Tales]; [13] [Magazine Addresses]; [14] [List of Individuals to Be Sent "The Battle That Ended the Century"]; [15] [List of Correspondents to Whom Postcards Have Been Sent]; [16] Suggested Recipients for Dragon Fly Outside Memb. List of NAPA; [17] Fungi from Yuggoth and Other Verses; [18] [Notable Stories in Recent Issues of *Weird Tales*]; [19] "Little Magazines"; [20] [Worthy Stories in Recent Issues of *Weird Tales*]; [21] [Pronunciation Guide]; [22] Tales of H. P. Lovecraft; Weird &c. Items in Library of H. P. Lovecraft; APPENDIX: [Advertisement of Revisory Services]; [Advertisement in the *New York Times*]; The Recognition of Temperance; [Advertisement in *Weird Tales*]; [Biographical Notice]; Preface [to *Old World Footprints*]; [E'ch-Pi-El Speaks]; Robert Ervin Howard: 1906–1936; Chronology of the Works of H. P. Lovecraft; Index of Titles (Volumes 1–5); Index (Volumes 1–5).

Notes. Cover illustration by Virgil Finlay, interior illustrations by Lovecraft. Hardcover 250 copies, Covington Group. Simultaneously published in hardcover and paperback. The fifth and final volume of the *Collected Essays*, with a cumulative index to all five volumes and chronological listing of all Lovecraft's work. For the CD-ROM of the set, see item 55.

37.   CLARK ASHTON SMITH. *The Complete Poetry and Translations, Volume 3: The Flowers of Evil and Others.* Edited by S. T. Joshi and David E. Schultz. 2007. 442 pp.

Contents. Introduction; *LES FLEURS DU MAL*, BY CHARLES BAUDELAIRE: Preface/Préface; SPLEEN ET IDÉAL: I. Bénédiction; II. The Albatross/ L'Albatros; III. Elevation/Elévation; IV. Correspondences/ Correspon-dances; V. [Untitled]; VI. The Beacons/Les Phares; VII. The Sick

Muse/La Muse malade; VIII. The Venal Muse/La Muse vénale; IX. The Evil Monk/Le Mauvais Moine; X. L'Ennemi; XI. Le Guignon/Le Guignon; XII. Anterior Life/La Vie antérieure; XIII. Travelling Gypsies/Bohémiens en voyage; XIV. L'Homme et la mer; XV. Don Juan aux enfers; XVI. To Theodore de Banville/A Théodore de Banville; XVII. Chastisement of Pride/Châtiment de l'orgueil; XVIII. Beauty/La Beauté; XIX. The Ideal/L'Idéal; XX. The Giantess/La Géante; XXI. Le Masque; XXII. Hymn to Beauty/Hymne à la beauté; XXIII. Exotic Perfume/Parfum exotique; XXIV. The Chevelure/La Chevelure; XXV. [Untitled]; XXVI. [Untitled]; XXVII. *Sed non satiata*; XXVIII. [Untitled]; XXIX. Le Serpent qui danse; XXX. Une Charogne; XXXI. *De profundis clamavi*; XXXII. The Vampire/Le Vampire; XXXIII. [Untitled]; XXXIV. The Remorse of the Dead/Remords posthume; XXXV. The Cat/Le Chat; XXXVI. The Duel/*Duellum*]; XXXVII. The Balcony/Le Balcon; XXXVIII. The Possessed/Le Possédé; XXXIX. Un Fantôme; XL. [Untitled]; XLI. *Semper eadem*; XLII. Tout entière; XLIII. [Untitled]; XLIV. Le Flambeau vivant; XLV. Réversibilité; XLVI. Confession; XLVII. The Spiritual Dawn/L'Aube spirituelle; XLVIII. Evening Harmony/L'Harmonie du soir; XLIX. Le Flacon/Le Flacon; L. The Poison/Le Poison; LI. Doubtful Skies/Ciel brouillé; LII. Le Chat; LIII. Le Beau Navire; LIV. L'Invitation au voyage; LV. The Irreparable/L'Irréparable; LVI. Causerie; LVII. Song of Autumn/Chant d'automne; LVIII. A une Madone; LIX. Chanson d'après-midi; LX. Sisina; LXI. Vers pour le portrait d'Honoré Daumier; LXII. *Franciscæ meæ laudes*; LXIII. To a Creole Lady/A une Dame créole; LXIV. *Mœsta et errabunda*; LXV. The Phantom/Le Revenant; LXVI. Sonnet d'automne; LXVII. Tristesses de la lune; LXVIII. The Cats/Les Chats; LXIX. The Owls/Les Hiboux; LXX. La Pipe; LXXI. Music/La Musique; LXXII. Sépulture; LXXIII. Une Gravure fantastique; LXXIV. Le Mort joyeux; LXXV. The Barrel of Hate/Le Tonneau de la haine; LXXVI. La Cloche fêlée; LXXVII. Spleen; LXXVIII. Spleen; LXXIX. Spleen; LXXX. Spleen; LXXXI. Obsession; LXXXII. Le Goût du néant; LXXXIII. Alchemy of Sorrow/Alchimie de la douleur; LXXXIV. Sympathetic Horror/Horreur sympathique; LXXXV. Le Calumet de paix; LXXXVI. A Pagan's Prayer/La Prière d'un païen; LXXXVII. The Cover/Le Couvercle; LXXXVIII. L'Imprévu; LXXXIX. Examination at Midnight/L'Examen de minuit; XC. Madrigal of Sorrow/Madrigal triste; XCI. The Adviser/L'Avertisseur; XCII. To a Malabaress/A une Malabaraise; XCIII. The Voice/La Voix; XCIV. Hymn/Hymne; XCV. The Rebel/Le Rebelle; XCVI. The Eyes of Bertha/Les Yeux de Berthe; XCVII. The Fountain/Le Jet d'eau; XCVIII. La Rançon; XCIX. Very Far from Here/Bien loin d'ici; C. Le Coucher du Soleil romantique; CI. On "Tasso in Prison" by Eugène Delacroix/Sur *Le Tasse en Prison* d'Eugène

MARIE RENÉ LECONTE DE LISLE: The Black Panther/ La Panthère noire; Ecclesiastes/L'Ecclésiaste; The Exhibitionists/Les Montreurs; The Howlers/Les Hurleurs; The Sleep of the Condor/Le Sommeil du condor; Solvet seclum; CHARLES VAN LERBERGHE: Song/Chanson; PIERRE LIÈVRE: Elysian Landscape/Paysage Elyséen [text not found]; The End of Supper/[title unknown; text not found]; STUART MERRILL: A Woman at Prayer/Celle qui prie; ALFRED DE MUSSET: Remember Thee/Rappelle-toi; Song/Chanson; SULLY-PRUDHOMME: Siesta/ Sieste; ALBERT SAMAIN: I Dream/[Untitled]; [Myrtil and Palemone]/ [Myrtil et Palémone]; FERNAND SEVERIN: Sonnet/Bois sacré; PAUL VERLAINE: IX (Ariettes Oubliées); Il Bacio; La Bonne Chanson; Crimen Amoris; En Sourdine; The Faun/Le Faune; Green; Moonlight/Claire de lune; Song from Les Uns et les autres; Spleen [Spleen]; To a Woman/A une femme; TRANSLATIONS FROM THE SPANISH: GUSTAVO ADOLFO BÉCQUER: Invocation/Rimas LII; The Sower/Rimas LX; Where?/Rimas XXXVIII; The World Rolls On/Rimas I (Libro de los gorriones); JOSÉ A. CAL-CAÑO: The Cypress/El ciprés; JOSÉ SANTOS CHOCANO: The Sleep of the Cayman/El sueño del caimán; RUBÉN DARÍO: The Song of Songs/El Cantar de los Cantares; JUANA DE IBARBOUROU: Rustic Life/Vida aldeana; JORGE ISAACS: Luminary/Luminar; JUAN LOZANO Y LOZANO: Rhythm/Ritmo; AMADO NERVO: Night/Noche; APPENDIX: XXVII. *Sed non Satiata*; LV. L'Irréparable; CXLI. Un Voyage à Cythère; The Peace-Pipe, by Henry Wadsworth Longfellow; Notes; Index of Titles; Index of First Lines.

Notes. Dust jacket illustration by Anastasia Damianakos. Published in a limited hardcover edition of 250 copies (Covington Group). The fruit of many years' work on the part of the editors. This volume, although designated Volume 3, appeared first because it was more convenient for the editors to issue Smith's translations of French and Spanish poetry than to prepare his original poetry (see item 50). Smith's translations (many of them in prose) and the original French and Spanish texts (chiefly from Baudelaire's *Les Fleurs du mal* but also from other poets such as Verlaine, Heredia, and Bécquer) are presented on facing pages. Many of Smith's translations are literal prose renderings that he had not yet versified. Most of the translations were previously unpublished. The recently discovered "The Desire of Loving," a translation of "Le Désir d'Aimer" by Hélène Picard, appeared in Volume 2.

38.   BARRY PAIN. *An Exchange of Souls.* HENRI BÉRAUD. *Lazarus.* 2007. 105 + 114 pp.

Notes. Cover illustration by anonymous (from the first edition of Pain's *An Exchange of Souls*) and by Ralph Fabri (Béraud). Part of the Lovecraft's

Library series. The first "Hippocampus double," analogous to the "Ace doubles" of the 1950s, in which two short novels were presented in a single volume. Pain's novel was first published in 1911 and manifestly influenced Lovecraft's "The Thing on the Doorstep"; Béraud's novel first appeared in French in 1924 (English translation 1925) and was an influence on Lovecraft's "The Shadow out of Time." Joshi has written separate introductions to both books.

39. PHILIP HALDEMAN. *Shadow Coast.* 2007. 255 pp.

Notes. Cover illustration and design by Cassie Barden; photograph by David Haldeman. A haunting novel of horrors in the Pacific Northwest.

40. *Dead Reckonings* No. 1 (Spring 2007). EDITED BY S. T. JOSHI AND JACK M. HARINGA. 100 pp.

Editorial; Knowing and Observing, by Paula Guran [David J. Schow, *Havoc Swims Jaded*; Glen Hirshberg, *American Morons*]; Cosmic Chess Games and Halloween Horrors, by Hank Wagner [F. Paul Wilson, *Harbingers*; Norm Partridge, *Dark Harvest*]; From Mr. Hands to Mr. Molester, by Tony Fonseca [Gary A. Braunbeck, *Prodigal Blues*]; Mommy Made Me Do It, by S. T. Joshi [Ramsey Campbell, *Secret Stories*]; Retropocalypse Now, by Michael Marano [Cormac McCarthy, *The Road*; James Newman, *The Wicked*]; Judgment Day, by Alan Warren [John Shirley, *The Other End*]; Strange Stories, by John Langan [Neil Gaiman, *Fragile Things*]; Ramsey Campbell, Probably; *Dandelion Wine* Redux, by Jim Rockhill [Ray Bradbury, *Farewell Summer*]; Pay No Attention to That Man Behind the Curtain, by June Pulliam [Brian Hodge, *World of Hurt*]; The Critic as Dadaist, by Richard Bleiler [John Clute, *The Darkening Garden*]; The Thing That Haunts the Dormitory, by Darrell Schweitzer [Alexandra Sokoloff, *The Harrowing*]; A Different Stephen King, by Ben Indick [Stephen King, *Lisey's Story*]; Weeding Out Emotion to Cultivate Violence, by Tony Fonseca [Jack Ketchum, *Weed Species*]; The Sheridan Le Fanu of Humor, by Steven J. Mariconda [T. E. D. Klein, *Reassuring Tales*]; A Remarkable Intellectual Figure, by Donald R. Burleson [H. P. Lovecraft, *Collected Essays*]; A New Dark Age?, by Rob Latham [J. G. Ballard, *Kingdom Come*]; Shades of Blackwood and Elgar, by Mike Ashley [Phil Rickman, *The Remains of an Altar*]; Twenty-First-Century Ghosts, by Stefan Dziemianowicz [Joe Hill, *20th-Century Ghosts*; Joe Hill, *Heart-Shaped Box*]; Books into Film and Vice Versa, by Matt Cardin [Tom Piccirilli, *The Dead Letters*; Tim Waggoner, *Darkness Wakes*]; Metaphysical Labyrinths and Fairy-Tale Archetypes, by John Langan [Tim Powers, *Three Days to Never*; John Connolly, *The Book of Lost Things*]; Lights, Camera, Horror, by Jack M. Haringa [Stephen

Graham Jones, *Demon Theory*; Mick Garris, *Development Hell*]; A Catalogue of Nightmares, by Robert Morrish [S. T. Joshi, ed., *Icons of Horror and the Supernatural*]; Capsule Reviews.

Notes. Cover illustration by Jason C. Eckhardt (uniform, aside from color, in all subsequent issues). The first issue of Hippocampus's review magazine, designed to carry on the wake of the defunct *Necrofile* (1991–99), published by Necronomicon Press. It was our feeling that the horror field needed a venue for substantial, thoughtful reviews of contemporary publications. Ramsey Campbell graciously allowed the reprinting of his column, "Ramsey Campbell, Probably," originally published in *Necrofile* and subsequently running in *All Hallows*.

41. S. T. JOSHI AND ROSEMARY PARDOE, EDITORS. *Warnings to the Curious: A Sheaf of Criticism on M. R. James.* 2007. 338 pp.

Contents. Introduction, by S. T. Joshi; I. SOME NOTES ON BIOGRAPHY: Montague Rhodes James 1862–1936, by Stephen Gaselee; Montague Rhodes James, by Shane Leslie; The Strangeness Present: M. R. James's Suffolk, by Norman Scarfe; M. R. James and Livermere, by Michael Cox; II. GENERAL STUDIES: Supernatural Horror in Literature, by H. P. Lovecraft; The Art of Montague James, by Mary Butts; The Ghost Stories of Montague Rhodes James, by L. J. Lloyd; The Toad in the Study: M. R. James, H. P. Lovecraft, and Forbidden Knowledge, by Simon MacCulloch; III. SOME SPECIAL TOPICS: On Not Letting Them Lie: Moral Significance in the Ghost Stories of M. R. James, by Michael A. Mason; Dark Devotions: M. R. James and the Magical Tradition, by Ron Weighell; M. R. James's Women, by David G. Rowlands; "The Rules of Folklore" in the Ghost Stories of M. R. James, by Jacqueline Simpson; "A Warning to the Curious": Victorian Science and the Awful Unconscious in M. R. James's Ghost Stories, by Brian Cowlishaw; "They've Got Him! In the Trees!" M. R. James and Sylvan Dread, by Steve Duffy; Homosexual Panic and the English Ghost Story: M. R. James and Others, by Mike Pincombe; "If I'm Not Careful": Innocents and Not-So-Innocents in the Stories of M. R. James, by John Alfred Taylor; "As Time Goes On I See a Shadow Coming": M. R. James's Grammar of Terror, by Steven J. Mariconda; "What Is This That I Have Done?" The Scapegoat Figure in the Stories of M. R. James, by Scott Connors; IV. STUDIES OF INDIVIDUAL TALES: The Nature of the Beast: The Demonology of "Canon Alberic's Scrap-book," by Helen Grant; A Haunting Presence, by C. E. Ward; "A Wonderful Book": George MacDonald and "The Ash-Tree," by Rosemary Pardoe; Who Was Count Magnus? Notes towards an Identification, by Rosemary Pardoe; A Haunting Vision: M. R. James and the Ashridge Stained Glass, by

Nicholas Connell; A Maze of Secrets in a Story by M. R. James, by Martin Hughes; Thin Ghosts: Notes toward a Jamesian Rhetoric, by Jim Rockhill; Nightmares of Punch and Judy in Ruskin and M. R. James, by Roger Craik; An Elucidation (?) of the Plot of M. R. James's "Two Doctors," by Lance Arney; Landmarks and Shrieking Ghosts, by Jacqueline Simpson; Addendum by Rosemary Pardoe; Bibliography; Acknowledgments; Index.

Notes. Cover illustration by Carl Wilton, from *Ghost Stories of an Antiquary* by M. R. James (London: Pan Books, 1953). The first volume ever published that was devoted solely to James's ghost stories. A substantial anthology, including both reprinted pieces (many from *Ghosts & Scholars,* the leading organ of M. R. James studies) and original works.

42.　FRANKLYN SEARIGHT. *Lair of the Dreamer: A Cthulhu Mythos Omnibus.* 2007. 307 pp.

Contents. Tainted Lineage, by Robert M. Price; There Is a Pond; Interlude at the Bridge; The Sorcerer's Pipe; The Innsmouth Head; Armillaria; The Guardian of the Pit; The Closing of the Gate; Mists of Death; Stomach Pains; Lair of the Dreamer.

Notes. Cover and interior illustrations by Robert H. Knox. Substantial collection of the Cthulhu Mythos fiction of Franklyn Searight, son of Richard F. Searight, a correspondent of Lovecraft. Includes the short novel of the title, previously unpublished.

43.　SEAN DONNELLY, EDITOR. *W. Paul Cook: The Wandering Life of a Yankee Printer.* 2007. x, 237 pp.

Contents. Preface; Acknowledgments; ABOUT W. PAUL COOK: W. Paul Cook: "An Ordinary Printer," by Sean Donnelly; Recollections of W. Paul Cook, by Arthur H. Goodenough; The Birth of Drift, by Walter John Coates; The Colossus of the North, by Edward H. Cole; In Memoriam: W. Paul Cook, by Edward H. Cole; A Bibliography of W. Paul Cook, by Sean Donnelly; BY W. PAUL COOK: John DeMorgan; By and about Ourselves; Inconsequentialities; First Impressions; A Thought; Howard P. Lovecraft's Fiction; H. P. Lovecraft; Introducing Vermont Names; More about Names; A Plea for Lovecraft; The Great "What Is It?"; Jim Morton; A Day in the Life of Willis T. Crossman; PROTEST STUFF: Introduction; Rhyme; Futility; Paternalism; The Root; Extermination; Parasites; The Plan; Mission; Confidence; Boomerang; The Butt; Fealty; Vacation; Tabloid; "Not Molested"; Amusement; The Parting; Joy Street; Church; Selections from *Contradictions* (Escape; Rootless; Easter; Awakening; Agnosticism); Waters of Lethe; About the

Editor; About the Book; *The Recluse* (cover) (1927); Photograph of Orton, Coates, and Cook; *In Memoriam: Howard Phillips Lovecraft* (cover) (1941); *Monadnock Monthly* (cover) (November 1901); *Vagrant* (cover) (Spring 1927); *A Day in the Life of Willis T. Crossman* (cover) (1934); *Protest Stuff* (title page) (1934).

Notes. Cover illustration by Gale Mueller. A lengthy biographical study of Cook, the amateur printer and close friend of Lovecraft. Also includes memoirs of Cook by his colleagues, a bibliography of his publications, and a rich sampling of Cook's prose and poetic writings. A companion volume to Donnelly's *Willis T. Crossman's Vermont: Stories by W. Paul Cook* (University of Tampa Press, 2005).

44. *Lovecraft Annual* No. 1 (2007). EDITED BY S. T. JOSHI. 160 pp.

Contents. Lovecraft Read This, by Darrell Schweitzer; Lovecraft and Lawrence Face the Hidden Gods: Transformations of Pan in "The Colour out of Space" and *St. Mawr*, by Robert H. Waugh; Memories of Sonia H. Greene Davis, by Martin H. Kopp; Letters to Lee McBride White, by H. P. Lovecraft (ed. S. T. Joshi and David E. Schultz); The Negative Mystics of the Mechanistic Sublime: Walter Benjamin and Lovecraft's Cosmicism, by Jeff Lacy and Steven J. Zani; Unity in Diversity: *Fungi from Yuggoth* as a Unified Setting, by Phillip A. Ellis; "They Have Conquered Dream": A. Merritt's "The Face in the Abyss" and H. P. Lovecraft's "The Mound," by Peter Levi; The Master's Eyes Shining with Secrets: H. P. Lovecraft's Influence on Thomas Ligotti, by Matt Cardin; Thomas Ligotti's Metafictional Mapping: The Allegory of "The Last Feast of Harlequin," by John Langan; Reviews; Briefly Noted.

Notes. Cover illustration by Allen Koszowski (uniform, aside from color, in all subsequent issues). The first issue of Hippocampus's scholarly journal devoted to Lovecraft, intended as a replacement of the defunct *Lovecraft Studies* (1979–2005), published by Necronomicon Press.

45. *Dead Reckonings* No. 2 (Fall 2007). EDITED BY S. T. JOSHI AND JACK M. HARINGA. 117 pp.

Contents. The World Down Under, by Sherry Austin [Ekaterina Sedia, *The Secret History of Moscow*]; A Cannibal's Boyhood, by June Pulliam [Thomas Harris, *Hannibal Rising*]; Poe, Poe, and More Poe, by Ben Fisher [Christopher Conlon, *Poe's Lighthouse*; James Robert Smith and Stephen Mark Rainey, ed., *Evermore*]; Green Glows and Trickster Gods, by Tony Fonseca [Thomas Tessier, *Wicked Things*; Philip Haldeman, *Shadow Coast*]; The Ultimate Clark Ashton Smith, by Hubert Van Calenbergh [Clark Ashton Smith, *Collected Fantasies*, Vols. 1 and 2];

Decadence in Verse and Prose, by Steven J. Mariconda [Clark Ashton Smith, *Complete Poems and Translations*, Vol. 3]; Tact and the Ghost Story, by Reggie Oliver [S. T. Joshi and Rosemary Pardoe, ed., *Warnings to the Curious*]; An Anatomist of Technoscience, by Rob Latham [Thomas Pynchon, *Against the Day*]; Ghosts and Scholars, by Brian Showers [Margaret Oliphant, *The Library Window*; Cheiro, *A Study of Destiny*]; Domination of Black, by John Langan [Laird Barron, *The Imago Sequence*]; Ligotti Redivivus?, by S. T. Joshi [Michael Cisco, *Secret Hours*; *The Traitor*]; Some Manifestations of Fantasy, by Ben P. Indick [Sean Wallace and Paul Tremblay, ed., *Fantasy*; Scriptus Innominatus, *Zencore!*]; Ramsey Campbell, Probably; Devouring Yet More Flesh, by Darrell Schweitzer [Kim Paffenroth, *Dying to Live*]; Ambrose Bierce's Moral Art, by Donald R. Burleson [*The Short Fiction of Ambrose Bierce: A Comprehensive Edition*]; Hardboiled and Haunted, by Jack M. Haringa; Tom Piccirilli, *The Midnight Road*]; The Yellow House on Benefit Street, by Scott Connors [Caitlin R. Kiernan, *Daughter of Hounds*]; Good, Bad, and Ugly, by Tony Fonseca [Peter Crowther, ed., *PostScripts 10*; Robert Morrish, ed., *Thrillers Two (II, 2)*]; Danger and Loss, by Paula Guran [Elizabeth Hand, *Illyria*; *Generation Loss*]; Memoirs, Essays, and Frivolities, by Richard Bleiler [Peter Straub, *Sides*]; Confronting the Unknowable, by Jim Rockhill [Lucius Shepard, *Dagger Key and Other Stories*; *Softspoken*]; Thrillers That Don't Thrill, by Michael Marano [Michael Marshall Smith, *The Servants*; *The Intruder*]; The Dark Delights of Gnostic Nightmares, by Matt Cardin [Richard Gavin, *Omens*]; Breathing Life into Old Plots, by Hank Wagner [Mary SanGiovanni, *The Hollower*; Sarah Langan, *The Missing*]; Unfinished Business, by Van Viator [John Farris, *You Don't Scare Me*; Lee Thomas, *The Dust of Wonderland*]; Open Mouths, Ready to Feed, by John Langan [Conrad Williams, *The Unblemished*]; Dudsville, by Alan Warren [Jeffrey Thomas, *Deadstock*; with Scott Thomas, *The Sea of Flesh and Ash*]; Enough Ghost Sex, Already, by Sherry Austin [Steve Berman, *Vintage: A Ghost Story*]; In the Garden of Yidden, by Ben P. Indick [Michael Chabon, *The Yiddish Policeman's Union*]; The Sounds of Violence, by Jack M. Haringa [Michael Arnzen, *Audiovile*; Elizabeth Monteleone, ed., *Dark Voices, Vols. 1, 2, 4, & 5*; Gruesome, *Johnny Gruesome*]; A Lasting Object of Contemplation, by Darrell Schweitzer [*Pan's Labyrinth* (film)]; The Darkling Plain, by Stefan Dziemianowicz; Capsule Reviews.

46. LELAND HALL. *Sinister House*. FRANCIS BRETT YOUNG. *Cold Harbour*. 2008. 108 + 161 pp.

Notes. Cover and interior illustrations by Haydon Jones (from the original edition of *Sinister House*) and by the anonymous artist of the first

American edition of *Cold Harbour*. Part of the Lovecraft's Library series. A reprint of two splendid novels discussed by Lovecraft in "Supernatural Horror in Literature." Neither *Sinister House* (1919) nor *Cold Harbour* (1924) appear to have had any direct influence on Lovecraft's stories, but further investigation may reveal subtle influences here and there. S. T. Joshi has written separate introductions to each novel.

47. EDITH MINITER. *Dead Houses and Other Works*. Edited by Kenneth W. Faig, Jr., and Sean Donnelly. 2008. xiii, 369 pp.

Contents. Introducing Edith Miniter, by Kenneth W. Faig & Sean Donnelly; ABOUT EDITH MINITER: Edith Miniter: A Life, by Kenneth W. Faig, Jr.; Mrs. Miniter—Estimates and Recollections, by H. P. Lovecraft; Edith Miniter, by Edward H. Cole; My Recollections, by William R. Murphy; Memories and Impressions, by Ernest A. Edkins; As I Knew Her, by Arthur H. Goodenough; Some Thoughts of Edith Miniter, by James P. Morton; My Friend Edith Miniter, by Nelson Glazier Morton; My Association with Edith May Miniter, by Truman J. Spencer; Edith Miniter, by H. P. Lovecraft; AMATEUR JOURNALISM: Salutatory; Editorial; Definitions Definitely Defined; Some Benefits of Amateur Journalism: A Hallowe'en Invitation; Hallowe'en Happenings; The Aftermath; Epgephi Musings; Falco Ossifracus; My Mother as She Seemed to Me; The Aftermath; The February Meeting; The Big Event; FICTION: To Thine Own Heart Be True; A Tragedy of the Hills; A Shadow on the Water; The Homecoming of Cleora; He That Will Not When He May: A Tale of Christmas Time; Wonted Fires; The Root of Age; The Emancipation of Elivra; Utilizing a By-Product; A Bunch of Crocuses; Aunt Ann's Bed; Cinderella Soapman; Nobody Home; Tartar Sauce; Thumbs; Dead Houses; About the Editors; About the Book.

Notes. Cover design by Sean Donnelly. A generous selection of Miniter's writings, including both fiction and amateur journalism. Miniter was a leading figure in the amateur journalism movement of the late 19th and early 20th centuries, and her fiction also appeared professionally. The book contains a lengthy biographical introduction by Faig and memoirs of Miniter by friends and colleagues, including Lovecraft.

48. DONALD WANDREI. *Sanctity and Sin: The Collected Poems and Prose Poems of Donald Wandrei*. Edited by S. T. Joshi. 2008. 195 pp.

Contents. Introduction, by S. T. Joshi; ECSTASY AND OTHER POEMS: The Voice of Beauty; Song of Autumn; Ecstasy; Let Us Love To-night; Vain Warning; On Some Drawings; Sanctity and Sin; To Myrrhiline; Song of Oblivion; In Mandrikor; The Woodland Pool; Death and the Poet: A Fragment; Satiation; In Memoriam: George Sterling; Bacchana-

Sound"; An Epitaph on Jupiter; Commentary; Index of Titles; Index of First Lines.

Notes. Cover and interior illustrations by Howard Wandrei. An exhaustive revision of Joshi's edition of Wandrei's *Collected Poems* (Necronomicon Press, 1988), augmented by several new poems and a sheaf of Wandrei's prose poems.

49. CLARK ASHTON SMITH. *The Hashish-Eater.* Edited, with notes, &c., by Donald Sidney-Fryer. 2008. 59 pp.

Contents. A Wind from the Unknown, by Ron Hilger; About Clark Ashton Smith and *The Hashish-Eater*; The Crystals, by Clark Ashton Smith; Argument of *The Hashish-Eater*, by Clark Ashton Smith; The Face from Infinity, by Clark Ashton Smith; Excerpt from a letter by Smith, summer 1950; The Hashish-Eater; or, The Apocalypse of Evil, by Clark Ashton Smith; Commentary; The Final Image; Suggested Interpretation; Conclusion.

Notes. Cover illustration by Clark Ashton Smith. Expanded from the editor's privately printed booklet (1990). Offered free with purchase of Smith's *Complete Poetry and Translations*; eventually made available for separate purchase. Audio CD contains hidden tracks of the editor reading a selection of other poems by Smith.

A thoroughly annotated edition of Smith's longest poem (581 lines) by the leading authority on Smith. The text of the poem comprises the original appearance in *Ebony and Crystal* (1922) and Smith's revised version (dating to the 1940s) from his *Selected Poems* (1971) on facing pages.

50. CLARK ASHTON SMITH. *The Complete Poetry and Translations.* Edited by S. T. Joshi and David E. Schultz, 2008. 2 vols. (xxxix, 846 pp., numbered consecutively).

Contents. VOLUME 1 (*THE ABYSS TRIUMPHANT*): Introduction; THE VOICE OF SILENCE (1910–1911): Cloudland; The Fountain of Youth; The Road of Pain; Reincarnation; Lethe; A White Rose; Death; Companionship; Illusion; The Call of the Wind; The Expanding Ideal; Imagination; The Sunrise; Night; To a Yellow Pine; A Sierran Sunrise; The Sierras; The Wind and the Moon; Moonlight; The Altars of Sunset; To George Sterling; The Voice of Silence; Weavings; The West Wind; Before Sunrise; At Nadir; The Besieging Billows; The Butterfly; The Meaning; To the Nightshade; The Garden of Dreams; Ode to Matter; Ode to Poetry; The Pageant of Music; Autumn Dew; The Eclipse; The Falling Leaves; The Freedom of the Hills; The Hosts of Heaven; Ode on the Future of Song; The Suns and the Void; To George Sterling; Moods of the

Sea; Sonnets of the Seasons; Spring; Summer; The Wizardry of Winter; The Storm; To the Morning Star; The Flower of the Night; A Sunset; War; Wings of Perfume; The Island of a Dream; Autumn's Pall; The Music of the Gods; The Night of Despair; Somnus; At Midnight; The Fanes of Dawn; The Summer Hills; To George Sterling; The Wind-Threnody; The Voice in the Pines; Black Enchantment; The Burden of the Suns; The Castle of Dreams; A Dream of Oblivion; A Dream of Darkness; The Revelation; The Dream-God's Realm; Ephemera; The Eternal Gleam; Evening; The Harbour of the Past; In Extremis; Lost Beauty; Nature's Orchestra; The Past; The Present; The Future; Time the Wonder; The Palace of Jewels; The Past; The Potion of Dreams; The Power of Eld; Romance; The Song of the Worlds; Sonnet on Music; Sonnet on Oblivion; Sonnet to the Sphinx; Sphinx and Medusa; The Sphinx of the Infinite; The Tartarus of the Suns; The Temple of Night; The Throne of Winter; Time; To a Cloud; To a Mariposa Lily; To a Snowdrop; To Ambition; To the Crescent Moon; To the Morning Star; To Thomas Paine; To Thomas Paine; Twilight; The Twilight Woods; The Vampire Night; The Waning Moon; THE ABYSS TRIUMPHANT (1911–1912): Antony to Cleopatra; Poetry; The Last Night; The Eternal Snows; The Moonlight Desert; Nocturne; Ode to Music; The Dream-Weaver; Ode to the Abyss; Medusa; The Messengers; Chant to Sirius; The Horizon; A Dream of Beauty; A Live-Oak Leaf; Wind-Ripples; A Song from Hell; The Palace of Jewels; The Star-Treader; To George Sterling; The Dream-Bridge; The Nemesis of Suns; Retrospect and Forecast; The Song of a Comet; Said the Dreamer; Saturn; The Shadow of the Unattained; The Pursuer; Echo of Memnon; Nero; The Mad Wind; Finis; Ode to Light; In the Desert; The Return of Hyperion; To the Daemon Sublimity; Atlantis; Averted Malefice; The Balance; The Cherry-Snows; Copan; A Dead City; The Eldritch Dark; Epitaph for the Earth; Fairy Lanterns; The Fugitives; Lament of the Stars; Lethe; The Masque of Forsaken Gods; The Maze of Sleep; The Medusa of the Skies; The Night Forest; Nirvana; Ode on Imagination; Pine Needles; The Price; The Retribution; Shadow of Nightmare; The Snow-Blossoms; A Song of Dreams; The Song of the Stars; Song to Oblivion; The Soul of the Sea; The Summer Moon; To the Darkness; To the Sun; The Unremembered; White Death; The Winds; The Morning Pool; The Abyss Triumphant; The Last Goddess; Satan Unrepentant; The Titans in Tartarus; The Cloud-Islands; Remembered Light; The Sorrow of the Winds; Luna Aeternalis; [In the Ultimate Valleys]; The Nereid; A PHANTASY AT TWILIGHT (1913–1917): The Ghoul; The Land of Evil Stars; The Clouds; The Doom of America; Nightmare; The City of the Titans; Desire of Vastness; The Medusa of Despair; The Refuge of Beauty; The Years Restored; The Witch in the Graveyard; The Sea-Gods; The Ministers of Law; Decadence; Somnus; To Beauty; The City of Destruction; The Orchid of Beauty; A Phantasy of Twilight; Beauty Implacable; The Nameless Wraith; The Ancient Quest; Aspect of Iron; Beyond the Door; The Harlot of the World; Psalm to the Desert; Inheritance; Memnon at Midnight; The City in the Desert; The Blindness of Orion; The Mirrors of Beauty; The Flight of Azrael; Duality; Love Malevolent; Exotique; Alien Memory; Fire of Snow; In the Wind; Lunar Mystery; Moon-Dawn; The Mummy; Morning on an Eastern Sea; Reclamation; Afterglow; Nocturne; The Crucifixion of Eros; Suggestion; Arabesque; Belated Love; November Twilight; Desolation; Coldness; The Kingdom of Shadows; Give Me Your Lips; Strangeness; Impression; The Exile; Ave atque Vale; The Tears of Lilith; Alexandrines; Autumnal; THE WHISPER OF THE WORM (1918–1920): A Vision of Lucifer; Sepulture; Palms; Mors; Dissonance; Eidolon; Haunting; Image; In November; Memorial; A Precept; Requiescat in Pace; In Saturn; Winter Moonlight; Inferno; The Whisper of the Worm; The Chimera; Autumn Orchards; Disillusionment; Ode to Peace; Antepast; Ashes of Sunset; At Sunrise; Crepuscule; The Melancholy Pool; Mirage; Mirrors; The Motes; Recompense; Satiety; Triple Aspect; Twilight on the Snow; Fantasie; Song of Sappho's Arabian Daughter; Forgetfulness; Transcendence; To the Beloved; Laus Mortis; The Traveller; Ombos; The Absence of the Muse; Quest; Symbols; Heliogabalus; The Hope of the Infinite; Flamingoes; Rosa Mystica; For a Wine-Jar; To Omar Khayyam; Beyond the Great Wall; Ennui; In Lemuria; Solution; The Ghoul and the Seraph; Tempus; The Dials; Silhouette; To Whom It May Concern; Speculation; Ode to Aphrodite; The Oracle; A Memory; To a Northern Venus; In Alexandria; The Incubus of Time; Amor Aeternalis; THE HASHISH-EATER (1920); THE INFINITE QUEST (1920–1922): The Dream; Requiescat; To Nora May French; Psalm; A Psalm to the Best Beloved; Cleopatra; Nightfall; Ecstasy; Secret Love; The Hidden Paradise; The Infinite Quest; Exotic Memory; Satiety; Fawn-Lilies; Artemis; Plum-Flowers; Chance; Union; Song; Love Is Not Yours, Love Is Not Mine; Poplars; The Fugitives; The Song of Aviol; Song; The Love-Potion; The Song of Cartha; Chant of Autumn; A Fragment; ENCHANTED MIRRORS (1923–1926): Selenique; Semblance; Change; Don Juan Sings; The Nymph; By the River; Fashion; The Witch with Eyes of Amber; On the Canyon-Side; We Shall Meet; The Secret; Contradiction; Alienage; Moments; Exchange; Metaphor; The Wingless Archangels; A Valediction; Cocaigne; Forgotten Sorrow; Septembral; Afterwards; The Barrier; The Funeral Urn; Dolor of Dreams; Brumal; Autumn Orchards; Remembrance; Departure; Diversity; The End of Autumn; On Re-reading Baudelaire; Lemurienne; You Are Not Beautiful; December; The Pagan; A Meeting; Adventure; Transmutation; The Last Oblivion; To the Chimera; Immortelle; In Autumn; Estrangement; A

Catch; Consolation; The Temptation; Apologia; Incognita; Enigma; Query; Loss; Concupiscence; Maya; Dead Love; A Prayer; Enchanted Mirrors; Minatory; Interrogation; Madrigal; Sandalwood; October; The Envoys; Ode; Un Couchant; A Sunset; Un Madrigal; A Madrigal; The Saturnienne; Apostrophe; Chansonette; Idylle païenne; Idylle païenne; Retrospect and Forecast; Sonnet lunaire; Sonnet lunaire; À Mi-Chemin; À Mi-Chemin; L'Abîme; Le Cauchemar; Chanson de rêve; Le Cheveu; Éloignement; Exotique; La Méduse des cieux; To George Sterling: A Valediction; After Armageddon; JUVENILIA: [Untitled]; [Fragment 1]; [Fragment 2]; [Fragment 3]; [Fragment 4]; [Fragment 5]; [Fragment 6]; Benares; The Prayer Rug; The Rubaiyat of Seyyid; Sunrise; The Skull; The Orient; Time; To an Eastern City; Fortune; The Ocean; Allah; Arab Song; Arabian Love-Song; Bedouin Song; The City of the Djinn; The Desert; A Dream of Vathek; A Dream of Zanoni; Eblis Repentant; From the Persian; From the Persian; From the Persian; Haroun Al-Raschid; The Inscription; Jewel of the Orient; Jewel of the Orient; Kismet; Mohammed; The Muezzin; Ode from the Persian; Odes of Alnaschar; Omar's Philosophy; The Palace of the Jinn; The Prayer Rug; The Prince and the Peri; Quatrain; Quatrains; Quatrains; The Snare; Song; Quatrains on Jewels; The Diamond; The Pearl; The Turquoise; The Ruby; The Opal; Rubaiyat; Rubaiyat; Rubaiyat of Saiyed; The Seekers; Some Maxims from the Persian; Stamboul; Suleyman Jan ben Jan; The Temple; The World; Youth and Age; Zuleika; Asia; Aurungzeb's Mosque; The Burning Ghauts; The Burning-Ghauts at Benares; Dawn; Delhi; A Dream of India; The Ganges; Alchemy; The Book of Years; Courage; The Days of Time; The Departed City; A Dream; Fear; The Fear of Death; The Feast; Hate and Love; Hope; The Land o' Dreams; The Leveler; Love; The Lure of Gold; Mercy; The Moon; Perseverance; Poem [?]; Resignation; The River; The River of Life; Sea-Lure; The Sea-Shell; Silence; Solitude; Summer Idleness; To the Best Beloved; The World; [Fragment 7].

VOLUME 2 (*THE WINE OF SUMMER*): SPECTRAL LIFE (1927–1929): Les Violons; Au Bord du Léthé; The Nevermore-to-Be; Fantaisie d'antan; Canticle; A Fable; De Consolation; De Consolation; Simile; Trope; Venus; One Evening; Tristan to Iseult; Souvenance; To Antares; Song; Amor Autumnalis; Warning; Temporality; Chansonette; Chansonette; Credo; The Autumn Lake; Le Lac d'automne; On a Chinese Vase; November; Chanson de Novembre; Chanson de Novembre; Exorcism; Winter Moonlight; Connaissance; Harmony; Moon-Sight; Sonnet; Similitudes; Calendar; February; Variations; Sufficiency; Lichens; Vaticinations; Nyctalops; The Hill-Top; L'Amour suprême; L'Amour suprême; Alexandrins; Absence; Une Vie spectrale; Spectral Life; Seins; Les Marées; Paysage païen; Le Souvenir; Rêvasserie; La Mare; Le Miroir

49

des blanches fleurs; Le Miroir des blanches fleurs; The Dragon-Fly; September; Shadows; Evanescence; Fellowship; Ougabalys; Ineffability; The Nightmare Tarn; Cumuli; Refuge; SOME OLDER BOURN (1930–1938): Answer; Song at Evenfall; Jungle Twilight; Madrigal of Evanescence; Solicitation; An Old Theme; Psalm; The Pool; Revenant; A Dream of the Abyss; In Slumber; Necromancy; Outlanders; Dominion; In Thessaly; The Phoenix; The Outer Land; Day-Dream; Contra Mortem; The Cycle; Kin; Sanctuary; Simile; Le Refuge; Le Refuge; La Forteresse; The Fortress; Sonnet; Ennui; Adjuration; Song of the Necromancer; Rêves printaniers; Rêves printaniers; Amour bizarre; L'Ensorcellement; Le Fabliau d'un dieu; Orgueil; Sea-Memory; Farewell to Eros; Indian Summer; Mystery; Touch; To Howard Phillips Lovecraft; The Prophet Speaks; Desert Dweller; Requiescat; Wizard's Love; THE LAST AND UTMOST LAND (1939–1947): From Arcady; Ode; Sestet; Bacchante; Resurrection; Witch-Dance; Song of the Bacchic Bards; Anteros; Lamia; Interim; Sonnet; To One Absent; Silent Hour; Grecian Yesterday; But Grant, O Venus; Bond; Madrigal of Memory; "That Last Infirmity"; The Thralls of Circe Climb Parnassus; Dialogue; The Mime of Sleep; The Old Water-Wheel; Fragment; Yerba Buena; Consummation; Humors of Love; Town Lights; The Sorcerer to His Love; To George Sterling; L'Espoir du néant; Amor Hesternalis; "All Is Dross That Is Not Helena"; Future Pastoral; Wine of Summer; In Another August; Nocturne: Grant Avenue; Classic Epigram; Twilight Song; Supplication; Erato; Anodyne of Autumn; The Hill of Dionysus; Before Dawn; Amor; Interval; Postlude; Strange Girl; De Profundis; Midnight Beach; Illumination; Omniety; Even in Slumber; Moly; Cambion; The Knoll; For an Antique Lyre; On Trying to Read *Four Quartets*; Greek Epigram; Lines on a Picture; Alternative; Hymn; The Sorcerer Departs; Surréalist Sonnet; Paean; Do You Forget, Enchantress?; The Horologe; Parnassus à la Mode; Sea Cycle; Dancer; Nevermore; Reverie in August; Tin Can on the Mountain-Top; Some Blind Eidolon; The Pursuer; To Bacchante; Calenture; Copyist; Love and Death; Quintrains; Essence; Epitaph for an Astronomer; The Heron; Bird of Long Ago; Late November Evening; Mithridates; Mummy of the Flower; Nightmare of the Lilliputian; Passing of an Elder God; Poets in Hades; Quiddity; Someone; Dying Prospector; EXPERIMENTS IN HAIKU (1947): Strange Miniatures; Unicorn; Untold Arabian Fable; A Hunter Meets the Martichoras; The Limniad; The Sciapod; The Monacle; Feast of St. Anthony; Paphnutius; Philtre; Borderland; Lethe; Empusa Waylays a Traveller; Perseus and Medusa; Odysseus in Eternity; The Ghost of Theseus; Distillations; Fence and Wall; Growth of Lichen; Cats in Winter Sunlight; Abandoned Plum-Orchard; Harvest Evening; Willow-Cutting in Autumn; Declining Moon; Late Pear-Pruner; Nocturnal Pines; Phallus Impudica;

Stormy Afterglow; Geese in the Spring Night; Foggy Night; Reigning Empress; The Sparrow's Nest; The Last Apricot; Mushroom-Gatherers; Spring Nunnery; Nuns Walking in the Orchard; Improbable Dream; Crows in Spring; High Mountain Juniper; Storm's End; Pool at Lobos; Poet in a Barroom; Fallen Grape-Leaf; Gopher-Hole in Orchard; Basin in Boulder; Indian Acorn-Mortar; Old Limestone Kiln; Love in Dreams; Night of Miletus; Tryst at Lobos; Mountain Trail; Future Meeting; Classic Reminiscence; Goats and Manzanita-Boughs; Bed of Mint; Chainless Captive; California Winter; January Willow; Snowfall on Acacia; Flight of the Yellow-Hammer; Sunset over Farm-Land; Flora; Windows at Lamplighting Time; Old Hydraulic Diggings; Hearth on Old Cabin-Site; Builder of Deserted Hearth; Aftermath of Mining Days; River-Canyon; Childhood; School-Room Pastime; Boys Telling Bawdy Tales; Fight on the Play-Ground; Water-Fight; Boys Rob a Yellow-Hammer's Nest; Nest of the Screech-Owl; Grammar-School Vixen; Girl of Six; Mortal Essences; Snake, Owl, Cat or Hawk; Slaughter-House in Spring; Cattle Salute the Psychopomp; Slaughter-House Pasture; Field Behind the Abatoir; Plague from the Abatoir; La Mort des amants; Vultures Come to the Ambarvalia; For the Dance of Death; Berries of the Deadly Nightshade; Water-Hemlock; Felo-de-se of the Parasite; Pagans Old and New; Initiate of Dionysus; Bacchic Orgy; Abstainer; Picture by Piero di Cosimo; Bacchants and Bacchante; Garden of Priapus; Morning Star of the Mountains; Bygone Interlude; Prisoner in Vain; Epitaphs; Braggart; Slaughtered Cattle; The Earth; Miscellaneous Haiku; Illuminatus; Limestone Cavern; Maternal Prostitute; Ocean Twilight; Radio; Tule-Mists; IF WINTER REMAIN (1948–1950): Hellenic Sequel; No Stranger Dream; On the Mount of Stone; Only to One Returned; Sonnet for the Psychoanalysts; Avowal; Tolometh; If Winter Remain; Almost Anything; "That Motley Drama"; Pour Chercher du nouveau; Dans l'univers lointain; In a Distant Universe; High Surf: Monterey Bay; Isaac Newton; La Muse moderne; The Mystical Number; Pantheistic Dream; Rêve panthéistique; Poèmes d'amour; Sandalwood and Onions; The Dark Chateau; Don Quixote on Market Street; The Isle of Saturn; "O Golden-Tongued Romance"; Averoigne; Zothique; Le poéte parle avec ses biographes; The Poet Talks with the Biographers; Beauty; La Hermosura; Las Poetas del optimismo; The Poets of Optimism; El Cantar de los seres libres; Song of the Free Beings; ¿Donde duermes, Eldorado?; Where Sleepest Thou, O Eldorado?; Los Dueños; Dominium in Excelsis; Parnaso; Parnassus; Las Alquerías perdidas; Lost Farmsteads; Cantar; Song; Eros in the Desert; Dice el soñador; Says the Dreamer; Memoria roja; Red Memory; Dos Mitos y una fábula; Two Myths and a Fable; La Nereida; La Isla de Circe; The Isle of Circe; Lo Ignoto; The Unknown; Leteo; [Lethe]; Añoranza; Melancholia; El

Vendaval; El Vendaval; Farmyard Fugue; Didus Ineptus; Amithaine; Malediction; Shapes in the Sunset; Sinbad, It Was Not Well to Brag; El Eros de ébano; Eros of Ebony; THE DEAD WILL CUCKOLD YOU (1950); THE SORCERER DEPARTS (1951–1961): The Stylite; Two on a Pillar; Not Theirs the Cypress-Arch; Alpine Climber; Hesperian Fall; "Not Altogether Sleep"; Seeker; Soliloquy in a Ebon Tower; The Twilight of the Gods; Qu'Importe?; ¿Qué sueñas, Musa?; What Dreamest Thou, Muse?; Que songes-tu, Muse?; Ye Shall Return; Lives of the Saints; Secret Worship; The Song of Songs; STYES WITH SPIRES; In Time of Absence; Nada; Seer of the Cycles; I Shall Not Greatly Grieve; Geometries; Alchemy; Sacraments; Delay; Verity; La Isla del náufrago; Isle of the Shipwrecked; Thebaid; Saturnian Cinema; Dedication: To Carol; The Centaur; Lawn-Mower; Tired Gardener; High Surf; H. P. L.; Cycles; FRAGMENTS AND UNTITLED POEMS: Al borde del Leteo; Ballad of a Lost Soul; The Brook; Demogorgon; Despondency; The Flight of the Seraphim; For Iris; Haunting; The Milky Way; Night; The Night Wind; No-Man's-Land; Ode on Matter; The Regained Past; The Saturnienne; Sonnets of the Desert; The Temptation; To a Comet; To Iris; To Iris; To the Sun; The Vampire Night; [miscellaneous fragments]; Broceliande; [miscellaneous fragments]; Twilight Pilgrimage; [miscellaneous fragments]; Limericks; Ripe Mulberries; From "Ode to Antares"; From "The Song of Xeethra"; From "Song of the Galley Slaves"; From "Song of King Hoaraph's Bowmen"; From "Ludar's Litany to Thasaidon"; From "Ludar's Litany to Thasaidon"; APPENDIX: *Prospective Tables of Contents:* The Jasmine Girdle; The Jasmine Girdle and Other Poems; Incantations; The Abalone Song; *Translations:* The Desire of Loving [a translation of "Le Désir d'Aimer" by Hélène Picard; [Sandalwood]; Voices; Notes; Index of Titles; Index of First Lines.

Notes. Cover photo by Jack Newton (vol. 1) and Anastasia Damianakos (vol. 2). 250 hardcover copies per volume, printed by Covington Group. The first complete edition of Smith's original poetry, completing the set that began with the publication of vol. 3 (Smith's translations) in 2007 (see item 37). The edition was the product of decades of work by Schultz; Joshi contributed editorial guidance only at a late stage of compilation. The edition was based upon the manuscripts of Smith's poetry that form part of the Clark Ashton Smith Papers at the John Hay Library of Brown University; nearly 300 unpublished poems appear here for the first time. The texts have been extensively annotated and arranged in chronological order by date of composition, so far as that can be established.

51. PHILLIP A. ELLIS. *A Concordance to the Poetry of Donald Wandrei.* 2008. 462 pp.

Notes. Published in hardcover without dust jacket. A concordance to Wandrei's poetry, based on the texts established in *Sanctity and Sin* (item 48).

52. *Dead Reckonings* No. 3 (Spring 2008). EDITED BY S. T. JOSHI AND JACK M. HARINGA. 94 pp.

Contents. A Swift River of Allusion, by Jim Rockhill [Emma Frances Dawson, *An Itinerant House and Other Ghost Stories*]; The Novel as Tumor, by Michael Marano [Stephen King, *Duma Key*]; Exploring the Breadth of Weird Fiction, by June Pulliam [Ann and Jeff VanderMeer, ed., *The New Weird*; Ellen Datlow, ed., *Inferno*]; Die Laughing, by Stefan Dziemianowicz [Ramsey Campbell, *The Grin of the Dark*]; The Self, the Landscape, by John Langan [Conrad Williams, *The Scalding Rooms*; Conrad Williams, *Rain*]; An Opportunity Lost, by Mike Ashley [Ian Alexander Martin, ed., *The First Humdrumming Book of Horror Stories*]; Kitchen-Sink Naturalism, by Rob Latham [Christopher Barzak, *One for Sorrow*]; In, Between, and Around the Genres, by Bernadette Bosky [Peter Straub, *5 Stories*]; More (of the Same) Can Sometimes Be Less, by Tony Fonseca [John Everson, ed., *Sins of the Sirens*; Hank Schwaeble and Gary Braunbeck, ed., *Five Strokes to Midnight*]; Cthulhuism and Yog-Sothothery, by Steven J. Mariconda [H. P. Lovecraft, *Essential Solitude: Letters to August Derleth*; *O Fortunate Floridian: H. P. Lovecraft's Letters to R. H. Barlow*]; Lives and Deaths at the Edge of Noir, by Jack M. Haringa [Brian Hodge, *Mad Dogs*; John Connolly, *The Unquiet*]; Stormy Weather, by Ben Indick [Nicholas Royle, *The Appetite*]; Ramsey Campbell, Probably; Creeping Nihilism, by Alan Warren [Adam-Try Castro, *The Shallow End of the Pool*; Tim Lebbon and Lindy Moore, *Children of the New Disorder*]; The Sublime and the Ridiculous, by S. T. Joshi [Dennis Etchison, *Got to Kill Them All*; Ray Garton, *Slivers of Bone*]; Liebestod in Lower Manhattan, by John Langan [John Marks, *Fangland*]; Dystopia Now, by Matt Cardin [Thomas Ligotti, *Teatro Grottesco*; Paulo Bacigalupi, *Pump Six and Other Stories*]; Burn This Book, by Hank Wagner [Clive Barker, *The Painter, the Creature, and the Father of Lies*; Clive Barker, *Mister B. Gone*]; It's All in the Telling, by Gary William Crawford [Brian Showers, *The Bleeding Horse and Other Stories*; Reggie Oliver, *Masques of Satan*]; They Know Their South, by Sherry Austin [Beth Massie, *Homeplace*; Will Clarke, *The Worthy: A Ghost's Story*]; Dross in Translation, by Jack M. Haringa [Asa Nonami, *Now You're One of Us*]; Nice Mice, by Ben Indick [Susan Palwick, *The Fate of Mice*]; Heirs to the King?, by Kevin Dole [Brian Keene, *Dark Hollow*; Richard Dansky,

53

Firefly Rain]; Two Centuries of American Ghosts, by Richard Bleiler [S. T. Joshi, ed., *American Supernatural Tales*]; Winning the Resurrection Lottery, by Scott Connors [Stephen Mark Rainey, *Blue Devil Island*; Greg Lamberson, *Johnny Gruesome*]; Capsule Reviews.

53.   DONALD SIDNEY-FRYER. *The Atlantis Fragments: The Trilogy of Songs and Sonnets Atlantean.* 2008 (paper edition 2009). 549 pp.

Contents. The Atlantis Fragments: An Introduction, by Brian Stableford; SONGS AND SONNETS ATLANTEAN: THE FIRST SERIES: Introduction, by Dr. Ibid M. Andor; Avalonessys; The Crown and Trident Imperial; Atlantis; The Rose and the Thorn; Rose Escarlate; "O Ebon-Colored Rose"; Your Mouth of Pomegranate; As Buds and Blossoms in the Month of May the Rose; To Clark Ashton Smith; Pavane; When We Were Prince and Princess; The Crown and Trident; Song; "Thy Spirit Walks the Sea"; Recompense; To a Youth; Spenserian Stanza-Sonnet Empourpré; A Symbol for All Splendor Lost; The Ashes in the Rose Garden; To Edmund Spenser (1552?–1599); Rose Verdastre; Ave Atque Vale; Thaïs and Alexander in Persepolis; A Fragment; O Fair Dark Eyes, O Glances Turned Aside; The Cydnus; Golden Mycenae; Lullaby; *Minor Chronicles of Atlantis* (Proem, by Michel de Labretagne; The Hippokamp; The Alpha Huge; The River Called Amphus; The Amphus Delta; The Imperial Crown Jewels of Atlantis; The Atlantean Obelisk; The Garden of Jealous Roses; The Tale of an Olden Love; The Shepherd and the Shepherdess; Reciprocity; The Iffinnix; A Vision of Strange Splendor); Kilcolman Castle: 20 August 1965; Aubade; The Lilac Hedge at Cassell Prairie: 27 May 1967; Black Poppy and Black Lotus; The House of Roses; "The Musical Note of Swans . . . Before Their Death"; Green Sleeves; O Beautiful Dark-Amber Eyes of Old; The Forsaken Palace; For the *Shapes of Clay* of Ambrose Bierce; Connaissance Fatale; For the *Black Beetles in Amber* of Ambrose Bierce; Offrande Exotique; *Sonnets on an Empire of Many Waters*: Legend; I. Here, where the fountains of the deep-sea flow; II. Atlantis; III. Gades; IV. Atlantigades; V. Atkantharia; VI. Iffrikonn-Yssthia; VII. Atalantessys; VIII. Atlantillia; IX. Atatemthessys; X. At-Thulonn; XI. Avalonessys; XII. Poseidonis; XIII. The Merchant-Princes; XIV. An Argosy of Trade; XV. Memories of the Astazhan; XVI. A Letter from Valoth; XVII. No, not until the final age of Earth; *Commendatory and Dedicatory Poems:* To an Atlantean Poet, by Margo Skinner; Inspiration, by Ian M. M. Law; Secretest, by Fritz Leiber; To Gloria Kathleen; For Master Edmund Spenser: His Great Song; Preliminary Note, by Brian Stableford; Notes, by Dr. Ibid M. Andor; SONGS AND SONNETS ATLANTEAN: THE SECOND SERIES: Preface; An Enchantress out of Time; A Summoning of Shadows; Valediction; In an Atlantean Bath; Lo Primordial; Strength of

Dreams; Copán; Quo Vadis, California?; Our Lady of the Unicorn; Rêverie Gothique; The *Monodon monoceros*; Beyond Ultima Thule; Midnight Visitant; An Invocation; A Miracle in Miniature; Bialowieza; Farewell to Zita; *From the French of José-Maria de Heredia* (Oblivion; Pan; The Goatherd; The Shepherds; Hortorum Deus; On a Ruined Bust of Marble); Return of the Conquistadors; Enigma; Pale Fragile Unicorns; Fantaisie Médiévale; Illumination; Renewal; Epiphany; A Vision of a Castle Deep in Averonne; *Some Further Fragments from Atlantis* (Pharanos Descending; My Mind to Me an Empire Is; Likewise My Mind to Me a Cosmos Is; Re-ascension; Pharanos at Sunset; Oneiromancy; At the Outhanox); Beauty; Notes; SONGS AND SONNETS ATLANTEAN: THE THIRD SERIES: Foreword, by Terence McVicker; To a Dead City; Memorial; The Herdsman; Tropicality; Totem; Abandonment; Amaranth; Rapa-Nui; Pendant; A Game of Chess; The Chest from Otherwhere; Another Species of Epiphany; A Ballade of Prospero; The Reef of Coral; Discovery; The Bitch with Tits of Bronze; Codicil of Contradiction; *As One Jaguär to Another* (Or So You Say; The Warrior and the Jaguär; Well Met by Midnight; The Jaguär and the Astrologer; The Apprentice and the Jaguär; Quoctezu Bids Farewell; The Passing of an Astrologer; Epilogue); Cephalopod in Residence; Colossal Chambered Nautilus; Hippokampoi; *As One Seahorse to Another* (The Little Horses of the Ocean Sea; An Oldster Gives Advice; A Mating Dance by Sunlight; Labor and Deliverance; A Proper Mode of Life; A Ghostly Dance by Starlight; Dominium atque Apotheosis); Hadrian and Antinous; Pan and Priapus; A Ship Sails Out to Sea; Barcarolle; On Reading Edmund Spenser Once Again; Nine Happy Goldfish; An Archaeologist Uncovers the Past; Macabre Arabesque; The Scallop Shell; Triolets du Jour; A Villanelle Not à la Mode; Item: Ariel Sings; Ancestral Memory Revived; The Scroll; To a Conch; Of Some Eternal Realm; Past, Present, Future; Demeure Exotique; The Fugitives; The Music of the Spheres; To Rinaldo for Clark Ashton Smith; Forevermore the Rose; Tableau Sous-Marin; Predicament; Remonstration; Enlightenment; A Rendezvous with Pierrefonds; Rondeau of Winter; Rondeau of Summer; Pierrefonds, Poème en Pierre; A Ballade of Duality; Conundrum; Rondel of Time; Rondel of Space; The Ghost of a Dream; A Fanfare from Atlantis; Appendix; Index of Titles; Register of Subscribers.

Notes. Dust jacket illustration by Gordon R. Barnett. Interior illustrations by William Boddy and Lance Alexander. Paperback edition omits frontispiece of Elizabeth I and endpaper map illustrations by William Boddy. A combined edition of the three volumes of the author's *Songs and Sonnets Atlantean* (1971, 2003, 2005), a scintillating series of poems and prose poems influenced in part by Clark Ashton Smith (whom Sidney-Fryer knew during the latter stages of Smith's life), Edmund

Spenser, and others, but also reflecting Sidney-Fryer's vigorously original poetic work. Originally published in a limited hardcover edition by subscription (300 copies, printed by Covington Group) and subsequently issued in paperback.

54. H. P. LOVECRAFT AND AUGUST DERLETH. *Essential Solitude: The Letters of H. P. Lovecraft and August Derleth: 1926–1931* (vol. 1) and *1932–1937* (vol. 2). Edited by David E. Schultz and S. T. Joshi. 2008. 880 pp. (numbered consecutively).

Contents. Volume 1: Introduction; A Note on This Edition; Abbreviations; Letters: Volume 2: Letters; APPENDIX : One for the Black Bag, by H. P. Lovecraft; The Weird Tale in English Since 1890 [excerpt], by August Derleth; A Master of the Macabre, by August Derleth; H. P. Lovecraft, Outsider, by August Derleth; H. P. L.—Two Decades After, by August Derleth. Glossary of Frequently Mentioned Names; Bibliography; Index.

Notes. Cover illustrations (different ones for the two volumes) by David C. Verba. 250 hardcover copies, printed by Covington Group. The first complete publication of Lovecraft's letters to Derleth, including 50 or so extant letters by Derleth to Lovecraft. Exhaustively annotated, with an immense bibliography of the hundreds of literary works (including their own) discussed by the authors. The edition constitutes, informally, the commencement of Hippocampus Press's ambitious plan to issue the complete Lovecraft letters in book form.

55. H. P. LOVECRAFT. *Collected Essays* (CD-ROM). 2008.

Notes. An electronic edition of the five volumes of *Collected Essays* (see items 18, 19, 29, 30, 36). It includes both text and digital images of all 13 issues Lovecraft's *Conservative*.

56. *Lovecraft Annual* No. 2 (2008). EDITED BY S. T. JOSHI. 215 pp.

Contents. Dispatches from the Providence Observatory: Astronomical Motifs and Sources in the Writings of H. P. Lovecraft, by T. R. Livesey; The Sickness unto Death in H. P. Lovecraft's "The Hound," by James Goho; Queer Tales? Sexuality, Race, and Architecture in "The Thing on the Doorstep," by Joel Pace; "Clever Lines": Some Thoughts on Lovecraft's "Ad Criticos," by Phillip A. Ellis; "The Rats in the Walls," the Rats in the Trenches, by Robert H. Waugh; Knowledge in the Void: Anomaly, Observation, and the Incomplete Paradigm Shift in H. P. Lovecraft's Fiction, by Kálmán Matolcsy; H. P. Lovecraft and the Archaeology of "Roman" Arizona, by Marc A. Beherec; Reviews; Briefly Noted.

Notes. Cover illustration by Allen Koszowski. Of particular note is Livesey's immense and penetrating study of Lovecraft's knowledge of astronomy.

57.   JONATHAN THOMAS. *Midnight Call and Other Stories.* 2008. 258 pp.

Contents. Foreword, by S. T. Joshi; Eben's Portrait; The Weird Old Hole; The Returns of Johnny Mapleseed; Fingers of Stone; Conjurings and Celtic Holidays (A Thematic Set) (The May Day Melée, Explained; Doctor Farrell's Goddesses; Some Days Before Shadow Damsel; In the Wake of Bridget; Midnight Call); Damn the Wheelwright; The Road to Schwärmerei; McEveety among the Leisure Elect; The Judgment Birds; An Office Nymph; Another Psychic on Comp; Towbear to Hell; The Christmas Clones; Awakening of No Return; A Vampire Heart; Subway of the Dead; Graveside Friday Night; Dappled Ass; An Alternate History of Annette; Tendrils in Formaldehyde; Ariadne's Hair.

Notes. Cover illustration by David C. Verba. A substantial and well-received collection of stories by a writer who met S. T. Joshi when the latter was giving a lecture at Brown University. Joshi at once recognized Thomas's talent and encouraged him to assemble a collection. A few stories had appeared in Thomas's rare collection, *Stories from the Big Black House* (1992), but these were extensively revised; the other stories are previously unpublished.

58.   RAMSEY CAMPBELL. *Inconsequential Tales.* [Edited by S. T. Joshi.] 2008. 249 pp.

Contents. Truth or Consequences; The Childish Fear; The Offering to the Dead; The Reshaping of Rossiter; The Void; The Other House; Broadcast; The Urge; The Sunshine Club; Writer's Curse; Property of the Ring; The Shadows in the Barn; Night Beat; The Precognitive Trip; Murders; Point of View; The Grip of Peace; Only the Wind; Morning Call; Pet; Hain's Island; Bait; Snakes and Ladders; The Burning; A Play for the Jaded.

Notes. Cover and interior illustrations by Jason C. Eckhardt. A volume Joshi had been encouraging Campbell for years to compile. When Joshi assisted Campbell in publishing a bibliography of his writings, *The Core of Ramsey Campbell* (1995), he noticed that many of Campbell's stories remained uncollected, and Joshi at last prevailed upon Campbell to gather them for this volume. Two stories were previously unpublished. The self-deprecating title—modeled, perhaps, on T. E. D. Klein's *Reassuring Tales* (2007)—is Campbell's.

59. *Dead Reckonings* No. 4 (Fall 2008). EDITED BY S. T. JOSHI AND JACK M. HARINGA. 97 pp.

Contents. A Grab-Bag of Perverse Delight, by Donald R. Burleson [Thomas M. Disch, *The Word of God*]; Edge-of-Your-Seat Suspense, by Hank Wagner [Joe R. Lansdale, *Leather Maiden*]; An Epic and Long-Awaited Publication, by Donald Sidney-Fryer [Clark Ashton Smith. *The Complete Poetry and Translations, Volumes 1 and 2.*]; Dissecting Thomas Harris, by Bev Vincent [Benjamin Szumskyj, ed. *Dissecting Hannibal Lecter: Essays on the Novels of Thomas Harris.*]; A Slow-Moving Tsunami, by S. T. Joshi [Caitlín R. Kiernan, *Tales of Pain and Wonder*]; Horror on the Ice, by Rob Latham [Dan Simmons, *The Terror*]; "The Weird Old Hole" and Much More, by Sherry Austin [Jonathan Thomas, *Midnight Call and Other Stories*]; The Nightmares That Cling to Us, by John Langan [Ramsey Campbell, *Thieving Fear* and *Inconsequential Tales*]; Sometimes You Just Have to Gush, by Matt Cardin [Stephen Mark Rainey. *Other Gods*; Michael Shea. *The Autopsy and Other Tales*]; Ramsey Campbell, Probably; A Shadow Across the Heart, by Jack M. Haringa [Jack Ketchum, *Old Flames* and *Book of Souls*]; Faster Than You Can Read Them, by Ben P. Indick [Brian Keene. *Kill Whitey* and *Ghost Walk*]; Torture, Cannibalism, and Necrophilia, by Tony Fonseca [Bill Breedlove, ed. *Like a Chinese Tattoo*; Nick Mamatas and Sean Wallace, ed. *Realms: The First Year of Clarkesworld Magazine*]; Everyday Horrors, by Javier A. Martínez [Bentley Little, *The Vanishing* and *The Academy*]; Nightmares and Dreamscapes, by Robert Butterfield [Patrick McGrath, *Trauma*; Greg F. Gifune. *Dominion*]; Confessionals, by John Langan [Christopher Conlon, *Midnight on Mourn Street*; Graham Joyce, *How to Make Friends with Demons*]; Vampires Doing Good, by June Pulliam [Tananarive Due, *Blood Colony*; Jewell Parker Rhodes, *Yellow Moon*]; Only an Abundance of Horror, by Tony Fonseca [Weston Ochse, *Scarecrow Gods*]; Erotic Fantasies and Necromantic Mysteries, by Hank Wagner [Polly Frost, *Deep Inside*; Sarah Monette, *The Bone Key*]; The Departure of "Enigma," by Kevin Dole [Nicholas Royle, *The Enigma of Departure*]; Ambitious Reading and Ambitious Feeling, by Michael Marano [Steve Rasnic Tem and Melanie Tem, *The Man on the Ceiling*]; Put-Downable, But Pick-Upable Again, by Darrell Schweitzer [Alexandra Sokoloff, *The Price*]; A Gothic Landscape, by Jim Rockhill [James Doig, ed. *Australian Gothic: An Anthology of Australian Supernatural Fiction, 1867–1939*]; Retrospective Reviews: The Line of Terror, by Arthur Machen [Walter de la Mare, *On the Edge*]; The Weird Scholar, by S. T. Joshi; Capsule Reviews; Correspondence.

60. KENNETH W. FAIG, JR. *The Unknown Lovecraft*. 2009. 253 pp.

Contents. Lovecraft: Artist or Poseur?; Quae Amamus Tuemur: Ancestors in Lovecraft's Life and Fiction; Whipple V. Phillips and the Owyhee Land and Irrigation Company; Lovecraft's Parental Heritage; The Friendship of Louise Imogen Guiney and Sarah Susan Phillips; The Unknown Lovecraft I: Political Operative; The Unknown Lovecraft II: Reluctant Laureate; Lovecraft's "He"; "The Silver Key" and Lovecraft's Childhood; The Dream-Quest of Unknown Kadath; Lovecraft's Unknown Friend: Dudley Charles Newton; R. H. Barlow; Robert H. Barlow as H. P. Lovecraft's Literary Executor: An Appreciation; Some Final Thoughts for Readers of This Collection; Sources.

Notes. Cover design (incorporating a photograph of Lovecraft) by Barbara Briggs Silbert. The date of the Lovecraft photo was given as 1936, based on a notation on the back of the photo, though it seems to be the one Lovecraft describes in a letter to R. H. Barlow [January 15, 1935]: "Has Talman sent you any of the surprise snaps he took at the gang meeting? I've just got a partial set—& I fared worst of all! The young rascal caught me as I was looking upward & saying something which put my mouth in an utterly comic position . . . as if I were going to whistle or expectorate!" A small number of copies were printed lacking the "Sources" section, and a few made it into circulation before the error was corrected. A rich collection of Faig's biographical essays on Lovecraft, including his landmark monograph on Barlow, which had never been published in its entirety aside from a limited edition.

61. S. T. JOSHI. *Classics and Contemporaries: Some Notes on Horror Fiction.* 2009. 291 pp.

Contents. Preface; I. SOME OVERVIEWS: Arkham House and Its Legacy; The Haunted House; Professionals and Amateurs; Some Thoughts on Weird Poetry; Bram and Bela and Mary and Boris; What the Hell Is Dark Suspense?; The Small Press. II. CLASSICS: Algernon Blackwood: The Starlight Man; Arthur Machen: A Minor Classic; William Hope Hodgson: Writer on the Borderland; E. F. Benson: Spooks and More Spooks; A. M. Burrage: The Ghost Man; Herbert S. Gorman: Where Is the Place Called Dagon?; Andrew Caldecott: The Well-Crafted Ghost; Rescuing Shirley Jackson. III. CONTEMPORARIES: Les Daniels: The Sardonic Vampire; Dennis Etchison and His Masters; Thomas Tryon: The Return of the Posthumous Collaboration; Stephen King and God; Peter Straub and the Blue Pencil; Ramsey Campbell: Alone with a Master; Clive Barker: Weird Fiction as Subversion; David J. Schow: Zombies, Tapeworms, and Kamikaze Butterflies; Donald R. Burleson: Enmeshed in the Bizarre; Norman Partridge: Here to Stay; Thomas Harris: Lecter as Albatross; Thomas Ligotti: The Long and the Short of It; Michael Cisco: Ligotti Redivivus?; Sherry Austin: The Southern Ghost Story; Shades of Edgar and Ambrose. IV. SCHOLARSHIP: The Charting of Horror Literature; Classics and Contemporaries. V. H. P. LOVECRAFT: Some Lovecraft Editions; The Cthulhu Mythos; Lovecraft as a Character in Fiction; Some Lovecraft Scholarship (Barton L. St Armand; Donald R. Burleson; Peter Cannon; Robert M. Price; Kenneth W. Faig, Jr; Edward W. O'Brien, Jr; Robert H. Waugh); Index; Acknowledgements.

Notes. Cover illustration by Allen Koszowski, a playful homage to Virgil Finlay's famous drawing of Lovecraft in periwig and smallclothes (see item 18), with Joshi as the Old Gent. An extensive selection of Joshi's book reviews, chiefly from *Necrofile* but also from *Lovecraft Studies, Studies in Weird Fiction, Weird Tales,* and other periodicals. Although written over a span of more than two decades, the volume forms a kind of foretaste of Joshi's forthcoming comprehensive history of supernatural fiction.

62. ADAM NISWANDER. *The Hound Hunters.* 2009. 302 pp.

Notes. Cover illustrations by Armand Cabrerra. (There are no interior illustrations, despite what the copyright page says.) An original Cthulhu Mythos novel by Niswander, and a loose sequel to *The Charm* (1993) and *The Serpent Slayers* (1994), published by Integra. *The Hound Hunters* had been scheduled for publication by Integra in 1995, and bound galleys had been issued, but the publisher collapsed before the book could be published. Niswander has outlined a thirteen-volume series of novels adapting the Cthulhu Mythos to a southwestern locale; for the next volume in the series, see item 69.

63. R. E. SPENCER. *The Lady Who Came to Stay.* ARTHUR RANSOME. *The Elixir of Life.* 2009. 153 + 180 pp.

Notes. Cover illustration of *The Lady Who Came to Stay* reprinted from the Knopf edition of 1933; cover illustration of *The Elixir of Life* is a detail from *The Alchemist* by Sir William Fettes Douglas. Part of the Lovecraft's Library series. A reprint of two novels that Lovecraft read and may have been influenced by: Ransome's fabulously rare *The Elixir of Life* (1915) and Spencer's *The Lady Who Came to Stay* (1931). Joshi has written separate introductions to each work.

64. *Dead Reckonings* No. 5 (Spring 2009). EDITED BY S. T. JOSHI AND JACK M. HARINGA. 93 pp.

Contents. The Vampire as Action-Adventure Anti-Hero, by June Pulliam [Rio Youers, *Everdead*]; A Mask Made of Exposition, by Michael Marano

[Gene Wolfe, *An Evil Guest*]; The Pathetic and the Mundane, by Kevin Dole [Quentin Crisp, *Shrike*]; Mythos and More Mythos, by Martin Andersson [Richard L. Tierney, *The Drums of Chaos*; Asamatsu Ken, *Queen of K'n-Yan*]; Forget-Me-Nots?, by Tony Fonseca [Ronald Damien Malfi, *Passenger*; Peter Atkins, *Moontown*]; A New Jungle Book, by Hank Wagner [Neil Gaiman, *The Graveyard Book*]; Abandon All Preconceptions, Ye Who Enter Here, by Sherry Austin [Ellen Datlow, ed., *Poe*]; Williams *One*, Clark *Zero*, by Robert Morrish [Simon Clark, *Vengeance Child*; Conrad Williams, *One*]; Mini-collections from Major Talent, by Matt Cardin [Douglas Smith, *Impossibilia*; Mark Samuels, *Glyphotech and Other Macabre Processes*]; Ramsey Campbell, Probably; Listing Towards Horror Paralyzed by Discomfort, by Jack M. Haringa [*British Invasion*, ed. Christopher Golden, Tim Lebbon, and James A. Moore]; Passing the Baton, by Ben P. Indick [*New Dark Voices II*, ed. Brian Keene; Jeremy C. Shipp, *Sheep and Wolves*]; Genius Loci, by John Langan [Cherie Priest, *Fathom*]; Enter Ghost, by Bev Vincent [Stieg Larsson, *The Girl with the Dragon Tattoo*; David Wroblewski, *The Story of Edgar Sawtelle*]; The Lovecraft Cult, by S. T. Joshi [Kenneth Hite, *Tour de Lovecraft: The Tales*; Robert M. Price, *Blasphemies & Revelations*]; Two Unique Visions of Horror, by Robert Butterfield [Scott Nicholson, *Scattered Ashes*; Tony Richards, *Shadows and Other Tales*]; Living on a Powder Keg, by Bev Vincent [Joe Hill, *Gunpowder*]; Can You Murder a Dream?, by John Edgar Browning [Jeffrey Ford, *The Drowned Life*]; Doing Your Homework, by Hank Wagner [F. Paul Wilson, *By the Sword*]; Waking to Nightmares, by Jack M. Haringa [Paul Tremblay, *The Little Sleep*]; The Supernatural in Prose and Verse, by Donald R. Burleson [S. T. Joshi, *Emperors of Dreams: Some Notes on Weird Poetry*; S. T. Joshi, *The Rise and Fall of the Cthulhu Mythos*; S. T. Joshi, *Classics and Contemporaries: Some Notes on Horror Fiction*]; The Perfect Museum Edition, by Darrell Schweitzer [Henry S. Whitehead, *Passing of a God and Other Stories*]; The Weird Scholar, by S. T. Joshi; Capsule Reviews.

65. *Lovecraft Annual* No. 3 (2009). EDITED BY S. T. JOSHI. 206 pp.

Contents. Lovecraft and the Ray-Gun, by T. R. Livesey; What Is "the Unnamable"? H. P. Lovecraft and the Problem of Evil, by James Goho; Some Notes on the Topographical Poetry of H. P. Lovecraft, by Phillip A. Ellis; The Theme of Distance in the Tales of H. P. Lovecraft, by Lorenzo Mastropierro; Lovecraft's Avatars: Azathoth, Nyarlathotep, Dagon, and Lovecraftian Utopias, by Brandon Reynolds; Self, Other, and the Evolution of Lovecraft's Treatment of Outsideness, by Massimo Berruti; Some Notes on Lovecraft's "The Transition of Juan Romero," by Leigh Blackmore; "The Shadow out of Time" and Time-Defiance, by Will Murray; Poems Not in *The Ancient Track*, by H. P. Lovecraft (ed.

S. T. Joshi); Lovecraft and the Polar Myth, by John M. Navroth; Reviews; Briefly Noted.

Notes. Cover illustration by Allen Koszowski.

66. H. L. MENCKEN. *Collected Poems.* Edited by S. T. Joshi. 2009. 145 pp.

Contents. Introduction, by S. T. Joshi; To R. K.; The Four-Foot Filipino: A Ballad of the Trenches; The Tin-Clads; Joe and Bobs; Auroral; One Man Band; A Frivolous Rondeau; A Few Lines; The Roorback and the Canard; Chrysanthemum; Canzonette; [Untitled]; An Ante-Christmas Rondeau; The Dawn of Love; [Untitled]; Fidelis ad Urnum; [Untitled]; A Ballad of Impecuniosity; A War Song; A Madrigal; A Song for Autumn; Nocturne; An Ode to a "Stein"; The Filipino Maiden; A Rondeau of Two Hours; When the Pipe Goes Out; Thanksgiving Day; Adlai; A Dirge; A Bacteriologal Romance; To O. P. K.; And Now Comes Congress; The Man That Guards the Grub; A Ballad of Looking; Well Buried; The Orf'cer Boy; A Paradox; Madrigal; The Song of the Slapstick; An Old, Old Story; Love and the Rose; The Coming of Winter; Outside, Old Year!; To Isaackhanmofakhammeddovlet; The Boy and the Man; The Donation Party; To Kruger; A Rondeau of Statesmanship; In Eating Soup; Serenade; Im Hinterland; The Snow; A Ballad of Fierce Fighters; The Pantoum of Congress; To Mrs. Nation; In Vaudeville; A Slug of Pessimism; An Ode to Nelson A.; To G. W.; A Sonnet to a Wienerwurst; The Ballade of the Rank and File; To Wu Ting Fang, Envoy Extraordinary and Minister Plenipotentiary; On Phyllis at the Play; Theatrical Alphabet; April; Dawn; A Villanelle; The Transport Gen'ral Ferguson; Faith; The Spanish Main; The Rondeau of Riches; A Ballade of Protest; Preliminary Rebuke; The Song of the Olden Time; The Ballad of Ships in Harbor; The Violet; September; Arabesque; The Rhymes of Mistress Dorothy; Roundel; Within the City Gates; Il Penseroso; Finis; War; On Passing the Island of San Salvador; Starting for the Play; Good-By, Divine Sarah!; The Old Trails; The Ballade of Cockaigne; Song; Invocation; The Voices; APPENDIX: A Kruger, by Edmond Rostand; Notes; Index of Titles; Index of First Lines.

Notes. Cover design (incorporating a photograph of Mencken) by Barbara Briggs Silbert. Perhaps an odd publication for Hippocampus Press, as both the author and the work are well outside the realms of horror or fantasy fiction; but the press has always sought to issue collected editions of poetry, and Mencken's poetry contains substantial merits. Mencken himself issued only 33 of his poems in his first published book, *Ventures into Verse* (1903). The others (most of them published in various columns in the *Baltimore Herald*) are uncollected.

67.　JOSEPH S. PULVER, SR. *Blood Will Have Its Season*. 2009. 284 pp.

Contents. Foreword, by S. T. Joshi; Choosing; Carl Lee & Cassilda; A Line of Questions; PITCH nothing . . .; I, Like the Coyote; Blood Will Have Its Season; mr wind sits; The Prisoner; An American Tango Ending in Madness; Orchard Fruit; The Songs Cassilda Shall Sing, Where Flap the Tatters of the King; The Night Music of Oakdeene; Dogs Begin to Bark All Over My Neighborhood; Chasing Shadows; But the Day Is a Tomb of Claws; In This Desert Even the Air Burns; And She Walks into the Room . . .; a certain Mr. Hopfrog, Esq., Nightwalker; The Black Litany of Nug and Yeb; Erendira; An Engagement of Hearts; An Event Without Knives or Rope; One Side's Ice, One's Fire; A Spider in the Distance; PAIN; A Night of Moon and Blood, Then Holstenwall; Under the Mask Another Mask; W a t e r l i l i e s; Yvrain's Black Dancers; No Exit Sign; Lovecraft's Sentence; Midnight on a Dead End Street in Noir City; The Master and Margeritha; Hello Is a Yellow Kiss; The Faces of She; Good Night and Good Luck; Patti Smith, Lovecraft, & I; The Collector and the Hand Puppet; The Only Thing We Have to Fear . . .; The Corridor; Stone Cold Fever.

Notes. Cover illustration by Thomas S. Brown. A scintillating collection of weird and fantasy tales by Pulver, previously known to the public as the author of the Lovecraftian novel *Nightmare's Disciple* (Chaosium, 1999).

68.　H. P. LOVECRAFT AND ROBERT E. HOWARD. *A Means to Freedom: The Letters of H. P. Lovecraft and Robert E. Howard: 1930–1932* (vol. 1) and *1933–1937* (vol. 2). Edited by S. T. Joshi, David E. Schultz, and Rusty Burke. 2009. 1004 pp. (numbered consecutively).

Contents. Volume 1: Introduction; A Note on This Edition; Abbreviations; Letters; Volume 2: Letters; APPENDIX: With a Set of Rattlesnake Rattles; The Beast from the Abyss; Dr. I. M. Howard: Letters to H. P. Lovecraft; Glossary of Frequently Mentioned Names; Bibliography; Index.

Notes. Cover illustrations (different for the two volumes) by David C. Verba. Limited edition of 345 hardcover copies, printed by Covington Group. A project long in the works—the collected correspondence of Lovecraft and Howard over an intense six-year period. The wordage of Howard's letters exceeds that of Lovecraft's, in part because some of Lovecraft's letters do not survive. Many logistical and legal issues had to be resolved before the edition could be published.

69.	ADAM NISWANDER. *The War of the Whisperers*. 2009. 341 pp.

Notes. Cover illustration by Ron Leming. The fourth novel in Niswander's series of thirteen southwestern Cthulhu Mythos novels, and the second to be published by Hippocampus Press (see item 62).

70.	DAN CLORE. *Weird Words: A Lovecraftian Lexicon*. 2009. 568 pp.

Notes. Cover art by Howard Wandrei. An immense dictionary of words used by Lovecraft and other writers of horror and fantasy fiction, with examples and citations extending back to the Tudor era. A monument of scholarship—a kind of *Oxford English Dictionary* for weird fiction.

71.	MICHAEL ARONOVITZ. *Seven Deadly Pleasures*. 2009. 247 pp.

Contents. Foreword, by S. T. Joshi; How Bria Died; The Clever Mask; Quest for Sadness; The Legend of the Slither-Shifter; The Exterminator; Passive Passenger; Toll Booth.

Notes. Cover and interior art by Thomas S. Brown. A collection of short stories by a dynamic new writer, who had submitted his work to Joshi a year or so before. Much will be heard of Aronovitz in the future.

72.	NORA MAY FRENCH. *The Outer Gate: The Collected Poems of Nora May French*. Edited by Donald Sidney-Fryer and Alan Gullette. 2009. 254 pp.

Contents. Acknowledgments; Nora May French: One Still, Small Voice out of Time and Space; Sources; THE OUTER GATE: THE COLLECTED POEMS OF NORA MAY FRENCH: The Outer Gate; Rain; Best-Loved; The Rose; Between Two Rains; The Message; By the Hospital; "Oh, Dryad Thoughts"; My Maid of Dreams; Music in the Pavilion; Rebuke; In Camp; The Nymph; Vivisection; The Stranger; The Constant Ones; Instinct; The Lost Chimneys; San Francisco, New Year's, 1907; The Panther Woman; The Poppy Field; Poppies; You; Just a Dog; Mirage; Dusk; THE SPANISH GIRL; PART I: I. The Vine; II. The Chapel; III. The Garden; IV; V; VI; VII; PART II; I; II; III; IV; V; VI; VII; PART III: I; II; III; IV; V; VI; VII; VIII; The Garden of Dolores; Answered; Indifference; After-Knowledge; Be Silent, Love; Two Spendthrift Kings; Growth; Change; Wistaria; How Ends the Day?; My Nook; When Plaintively and Near the Cricket Sings; The Little Memories; Pass By; In Empty Courts; Down the Trail; "Bells from Over the Hills Sound Sweet"; In Town; Moods; A Misty Morning; Two Songs; Noon; Your Beautiful Passing; By Moonlight; A Dream-Love; One Day; The Mission Graves; Along the Track; A Place of Dreams; Think Not, O Lilias7; The Suicide; "To Rosy Buds . . . ."; Yesterday; The Mourner; Ave atque Vale;

At the End; Notes; NOTICES: General Note; San Francisco *Bulletin*, Friday evening, 15 November 1907; San Francisco *Call*, Friday, 15 November 1907; San Francisco *Chronicle*, Friday, 15 November 1907; San Francisco *Chronicle*, Friday, 15 November 1907, notes; San Francisco *Examiner*, Friday, November 15, 1907; Los Angeles *Times*, Friday, November 15, 1907; Los Angeles *Times*, Sunday, November 17, 1907; Los Angeles *Times*, Monday, 18 November 1907; *Town Talk*, Saturday, 23 November 1907; *Current Literature*, June 1908; San Francisco *Call*, Sunday, June 12, 1910; *The New Age, A Weekly Review of Politics, Literature and Art*, Thursday, 14 July 1910; *Current Literature*, September 1910; *Die Nieuwe Gids* [*The New Guidebook*], November 1910; Poems by Nora May French, *The California Literary Pamphlets*, Number 2; Helen (Augusta) French Hunt (1883–1973): A Little Memoir (A Friendship, 1968–1973); TRIBUTES: General Note; Sources; Untitled, by Henry Anderson Lafler; Sonnet, by Henry Anderson Lafler; Sonnet, by Henry Anderson Lafler; The Pearl, by Henry Anderson Lafler; Nora May French, by George Sterling; The Ashes in the Sea, by George Sterling; Nora May French, In Memoriam, by Louise Gebhard Cann; To Nora May French, by Clark Ashton Smith; "Thy Spirit Walks the Sea," by Donald Sidney-Fryer; [Nora May French], by Dorothy Jesse Beagle; For Nora May in Paradise, by Mary Rudge; Nora May, by Alan Gullette; For Nora May French, by Val Beatts; Quicksilver, by Do Gentry; November, by Do Gentry; The Poet Replies, by Do Gentry; Dear Critic, Dear Abstraction, by Do Gentry; The Poet with Us: Nora May French, by Marvin R. Hiemstra; Index of Titles; Index of First Lines.

Notes. Cover photograph of Nora May French by Arnold Genthe, cover design by Barbara Briggs Silbert. A landmark of scholarship: the editors not only unearthed numerous poems by French (1881–1907) not included in her lone posthumous volume, *Poems* (1910), but also included a generous sampling of reviews of that book along with other interesting matter. French was a beautiful and talented poet in George Sterling's literary circle who committed suicide at the age of 26. Her delicate and sensitive poetry retains a following to this day.

73. *Dead Reckonings* No. 6 (Fall 2009). EDITED BY S. T. JOSHI AND JACK M. HARINGA. 94 pp.

Contents. Crooked House, by Bev Vincent [Sarah Langan, *Audrey's Door*]; From the Sensuous to the Sophomoric, by Zachary Z. E. Bennett [David Niall Wilson, *Ennui and Other Stories of Madness*]; Ending the World: Do's and Don'ts, by Kevin Dole [Lavie Tidhar and Nir Yaniv, *The Tel Aviv Dossier*; Tim Lebbon, *Bar None*]; For Aficionados Only, by Robert Butterfield [Simon Stranzas, *Cold to the Touch*; Alan M. Clark and

Elizabeth Massie, *D. D. Murphry, Secret Policeman*]; Destined for the Remainder Shelves, by Scott David Briggs [Brian Knight, *Reservoir Gods*; Seamus Cooper, *The Mall of Cthulhu*]; The Way of Escape, by Sherry Austin [Barbara Roden, Northwest Passages; Kealan Patrick Burke, The 121 to Pennsylvania and Others]; More Than Just Tentacles, by Martin Andersson [Henrik Harksen, ed., *Eldritch Horrors*; Ellen Datlow, ed., *Lovecraft Unbound*]; Apocalypse Nowadays, by John Edgar Browning [Greg F. Gifune, *Children of Chaos*; Greg F. Gifune, *Blood in Electric Blue*]; Gold, Silver, and Bronze, by Hank Wagner [Stephen Jones, ed. *The Mammoth Book of Best New Horror 20*; Charles Black, ed. *The Fourth Black Book of Horror*; Richard Chizmar, ed. *Shivers V.*]; Ramsey Campbell, Probably: The Edited Version; Impalements at Piccadilly Circus, by John Edgar Browning [Dacre Stoker and Ian Holt, *Dracula the Un-Dead*]; Horror as an Afterthought, by Tony Fonseca [John Harwood, *The Séance*; Gemma Mawdsley, *The Paupers' Graveyard*]; Of Fishmen and Lovecraftian Place-Names, by John M. Navroth [James A. Moore, *Deeper*]; A Modern "Heart of Darkness," by S. T. Joshi [Caitlín R. Kiernan, *The Red Tree*]; The Banality of Evil, by June Pulliam [Bentley Little, *His Father's Son*]; Two (or More) Tales of Dark Religion, by Matt Cardin [Leopoldo Gout, *Ghost Radio*; Brian Evenson, *Last Days*]; Robert Bloch: *Psycho* and Beyond, by Henrik Sandbeck Harksen [Benjamin Szumskyj, ed., *The Man Who Collected Psychos: Critical Essays on Robert Bloch*]; Tradition Viewed through Different Lenses, by Jim Rockhill [Scott Thomas, *The Garden of Ghosts*; John Langan, *Mr. Gaunt and Other Uneasy Encounters*]; Formula and Geography, by Richard Bleiler [Graham Masterton, *Basilisk*; Danel Olson, ed., *Exotic Gothic 2: New Tales of Taboo*]; A Window onto the Real Poe, by Benjamin F. Fisher [John Ward Ostrom, ed., *The Collected Letters of Edgar Allan Poe*]; Vampires, the Holocaust, and 9/11, by Michael Marano [Guillermo del Toro and Chuck Hogan, *The Strain*]; The Weird Tradition in Poetry, by Darrell Schweitzer [Donald Wandrei, *Sanctity and Sin*; Rain Graves, *Barfodder*]; The Perfect Length for Horror, by Hank Wagner [Sarah Pinborough. *The Language of Dying*; Terry Lamsley. *R.I.P.*; Joel Lane. *The Witnesses Are Gone*]; The Weird Scholar, by S. T. Joshi.

Notes. The last issue with Haringa as coeditor. Subsequent issues are co-edited by Joshi and Tony Fonseca.

74. DONALD R. BURLESON. *Wait for the Thunder: Stories for a Stormy Night*. 2010. 300 pp.

Contents. Tumbleweeds; One-Night Strand; Hopscotch; Jigsaw; Country Living; Sheep-Eye; Tummerwunky; A Student of Geometry; Fwoo; Down in the Mouth; Crayons; The Weeping Woman of White

Crow; Spider Willie; Jack O'Lantern Jack; The Watcher at the Window; Desert Dreams; Grampa Pus; Gramma Grunt; Sheets; Up and About; Blessed Event; The Cryptogram; Leaves; Pump Jack; Lujan's Trunk; Wait for the Thunder; Papa Loaty.

Notes. Cover illustration by Thomas S. Brown. A substantial collection of stories by Burleson, who has established himself both as a leading literary scholar (especially of H. P. Lovecraft) and a short story writer and novelist. The volume includes stories published since the issuance of his previous collection, *Beyond the Lamplight* (Jack o' Lantern Press, 1996).

75. H. B. DRAKE. *The Shadowy Thing.* 2010. 245 pp.

Notes. Cover illustration taken from the 1928 A. L. Burt reprint of *The Shadowy Thing;* cover design by Barbara Briggs Silbert. Part of the Lovecraft's Library series. A reprint of the novel first published in the UK as *The Remedy* (1925) and in the US as *The Shadowy Thing* (1928). Lovecraft read it not long after publication, and it manifestly influenced "The Thing on the Doorstep" (1933). Contains an introduction by S. T. Joshi.

76. ROBERT M. PRICE, EDITOR. *The Tindalos Cycle.* 2010. 365 pp.

Contents: Chock Full o' Mutts (introduction), by Robert M. Price; The Maker of Moons, by Robert W. Chambers; The Death of Halpin Frayser, by Ambrose Bierce; The Space-Eaters, by Frank Belknap Long; The Hounds of Tindalos, by Frank Belknap Long; The Letters of Halpin Chalmers, by Peter Cannon; The Death of Halpin Chalmers, by Perry M. Grayson; The Madness out of Time, by Lin Carter; The Hound of the Partridgevilles, by Peter Cannon; Through Outrageous Angles, by David C. Kopaska-Merkel and Ronald McDowell; Firebrands of Torment, by Michael Cisco; The Shore of Madness, by Ann K. Schwader; Gateway to Forever, by Frank Belknap Long; The Gift of Lycanthropy, by Frank Belknap Long; The War Among the Gods, by Adrian Cole; The Ways of Chaos, by Ramsey Campbell; Juggernaut, by C. J. Henderson; Scarlet Obeisance, by Joseph S. Pulver, Sr.; The Horror from the Hills, by Frank Belknap Long; Pompelo's Doom, by Ann K. Schwader; Confession of the White Acolyte, by Ann K. Schwader; When Chaugnar Wakes, by Frank Belknap Long; The Elephant God of Leng, by Robert M. Price; Death Is an Elephant, by Robert Bloch; The Dweller in the Pot by Frank Chimesleep Short, by Robert M. Price; But It's A Long Dark Road, by Joseph S. Pulver, Sr.; Nyarlatophis: A Fable of Ancient Egypt, by Stanley C. Sargent; Mind-Pilot, by William Laughlin.

Notes. Cover illustration by Thomas S. Brown. A rich collection of stories (some of them parodies) playing off of the Hounds of Tindalos, as created in the story of that title by Frank Belknap Long.

77. THOMAS LIGOTTI. *The Conspiracy against the Human Race.* 2010. 219 pp.

Notes. Cover design and photograph of the author by Jennifer Gariepy; cover production by Barbara Briggs Silbert. Limited hardcover edition of 1150 copies, printed by Covington Group. For the first time, we also issued roughly 100 uncorrected proof copies in paperback, in advance of publication of the hardcover. A remarkable philosophical treatise by Ligotti, best known as one of the most dynamic and innovative writers of supernatural literature to emerge in recent years. The volume (which includes its share of literary criticism, including discussions of Lovecraft and other weird writers) is a searching examination of the fundamental wretchedness of the human race.

78. JONATHAN THOMAS. *Tempting Providence.* 2010. 261 pp.

Contents: Foreword, by Sherry Austin; Dead Men's Shoes; Into Your Tenement I'll Creep; Tempting Providence; A Different Kind of Heartworm; Gumball Man; The Silence in the Copse; The Lord of the Animals; The Salvage Saints; Passenger Bastion; Power of Midnight; The Men at the Mound; Three Ounces over Advent.

Notes. Cover illustration by Thomas S. Brown. The second collection of Thomas's short fiction featuring a number of richly evocative novelettes, following the well-received *Midnight Call* (see item 57). Most of the stories were previously unpublished.

79. *Dead Reckonings* No. 7 (Spring 2010). EDITED BY S. T. JOSHI AND TONY FONSECA. 120 pp.

Contents. Realms of Perilous Delight, by Jim Rockhill [Richard Gavin, *The Darkly Splendid Realm*; Matt Cardin, *Dark Awakenings*]; The Red and the Blue, by Scott Connors [H. P. Lovecraft and Robert E. Howard, *A Means to Freedom*; Robert E. Howard, *The Horror Stories of Robert E. Howard* and *Heroes in the Wind: From Kull to Kane*]; A Macabre Display, by Javier A. Martinez [Jeffrey Thomas, *Thirteen Specimens: A Collection of the Bizarre*]; The Evil That Lurks Inside Us, by Jonathan Johnson [Michael Aronovitz, *Seven Deadly Pleasures*]; The Eldritch and the Cosmic, by Martin Andersson [S. T. Joshi, ed., *Black Wings: New Tales of Lovecraftian Horror*]; Rain, Rain, Everywhere, by S. T. Joshi [Ramsey Campbell, *Creatures of the Pool* and *Just Behind You*]; My Dear Watson, It's a Zombie Raccoon!, by Tony Fonseca [Martin H. Greenberg and Kerrie Hughes, ed., *Zombie Raccoons and Killer Bunnies*; John Joseph Adams, ed., *The Improbable Adventures of Sherlock Holmes*]; Where's the Plot?, by Andy K. Trevathan [L. A. Banks, *Undead on Arrival* and "Ev'ry Shut Eye Ain't

Asleep"]; Living in a Topolganger, by Rob Latham [China Miéville, *The City & ytiC ehT*]; B-Grade and Z-Grade, by Matt Cardin [Richard Laymon, *Flesh* and *Dark Mountain*]; Lesser Straub, But Still Worth Reading, by Richard Bleiler [Peter Straub, *A Dark Matter*]; Ramsey Campbell, Probably: Restyling for Our Time; Bloodbath and Mayhem, by Lisa Nunn [Graham Masterton, *Death Mask* and *Blind Panic*]; Road Dogs and Iron Dead, by S. T. Joshi [Norman Partridge, *Lesser Demons*]; Horrors Down Under, by Leigh Blackmore [Felicity Dowker, *Phantasy Made Grotesk*; Robert Hood, *Creeping in Reptile Flesh*]; The Dead Return and They Have Bite, by Van Viator [Edward Lee, *The Golem*; Ray Garton, *Bestial*]; Less Artful Than Enthusiastic, by Robert Butterfield [Gord Rollo, *Crimson* and *Strange Magic*]; All That Glitters . . ., by Kevin Dole [Ellen Datlow, ed., *The Best Horror of the Year, Volume One*; William F. Nolan and Jason V Brock, ed., *The Bleeding Edge*]; Post-Columbine and the Gothic, by John Edgar Browning [Gary A. Braunbeck, *Far Dark Fields*]; Cautionary Tales, by Antoinette Winstead [Dean R. Koontz, *Dean Koontz's Frankenstein: Dead and Alive*; Conrad Williams, *Decay Inevitable*]; A Matheson Sampler, by Darrell Schweitzer [Richard Matheson, *The Box*]; The Permeability of Flesh, by Vicky Gilpin [Brian Keene, *Castaways* and *Urban Gothic*]; Lycanthropes and Rotters, by Kendra Kuss Ditto [Laurell K. Hamilton, *Skin Trade*; Cherie Priest, *Boneshaker*]; Scarifyingly Assured, by Matt Cardin [John Langan, *House of Windows*]; Weaponized Affluence, by Michael Marano [Suzanne Collins, *The Hunger Games* and *Catching Fire*]; Skipping the Light Fandango, by Melissa Ursula Dawn Goldsmith [Michael Long, *Beautiful Monsters: Imagining the Classic in Musical Media*]; Cthulhu in San Francisco, by Scott David Briggs [Michael Shea, *Copping Squid and Other Mythos Tales*]; Capsule Reviews.

80. S. T. JOSHI. *I Am Providence: The Life and Times of H. P. Lovecraft.* 2010. 2 vols. x, 1151 pp. (numbered consecutively).

Notes. Cover illustrations consist of photographs of H. P. Lovecraft (different for each volume). Unabridged and updated version of Joshi's *H. P. Lovecraft: A Life* (Necronomicon Press, 1996), with more than 150,000 words restored to the text and much of it brought up to date to take account of recent discoveries in Lovecraft's life and work. Published in a limited hardcover edition (1000 copies) by subscription.

81. *Lovecraft Annual* No. 4 (2010). EDITED BY S. T. JOSHI. 206 pp.

Contents. Lovecraft's "The Bride of the Sea" and the Uses of Bathos, by Manuel Pérez-Campos; Following "The Ancient Track," by Jonathan Adams (includes musical composition, "The Ancient Track," by Adams); Letters to Carl Ferdinand Strauch, by H. P. Lovecraft; Appendix: A Library Goes Regionalist, by Carl F. Strauch; The Construction of Race in the Early Poetry of H. P. Lovecraft, by Phillip A. Ellis; The Ecstasies of "The Thing on the Doorstep," "Medusa's Coil," and Other Erotic Studies by Robert H. Waugh; Notes on a Nonentity, by H. P. Lovecraft; In Memoriam: Dr. Harry K. Brobst (1909–2010), by Christopher M. O'Brien; Time, Space, and Natural Law: Science and Pseudo-Science in Lovecraft, by S. T. Joshi; Reviews; Briefly Noted.

Notes. Cover illustration by Allen Koszowski. Of note are the lengthy and penetrating discussion of Lovecraft's poetry by Pérez-Campos and the musical setting of "The Ancient Track" by Adams, a professional composer.

82. *Dead Reckonings* No. 8 (Fall 2010). EDITED BY S. T. JOSHI AND TONY FONSECA. 114 pp.

Notes. His Best in Years: King in Fine Form, by Hank Wagner [Stephen King, *Just After Sunset*; Stephen King, *Under the Dome*]; A Sheaf of Horrific Delights, by Leigh Blackmore [Richard L. Tierney, *Savage Menace and Other Poems*]; Motels, Arachnids, and High Heels, by Scott David Briggs [Donald R. Burleson, *Wait for the Thunder*]; Custer's Last Stand, by Bev Vincent [Dan Simmons, *Black Hills*]; Is the Soul Changeless?, by Kendra Ditto [Michael Schiefelbein, *Vampire Maker*; Gail Carriger, *Changeless*]; Doubly Disappointing, by Tony Fonseca [Robert R. McCammon, *Mystery Walk*; Jeffrey Thomas, *Thought Forms*]; Horrors Cosmic and Personal, by Javier A. Martínez [Brian Keene, *Darkness on the Edge of Town*; Ray Garton, *Scissors*]; On the Rack, by Michael Marano [Michael Marshall Smith, *What Happens When You Wake Up in the Night*; Tom Fletcher, *The Safe Children*; Joel Lane, *Black Country*; Alison Moore, *When the Door Closed, It Was Dark*]; A Portrait of the Artist, by Steven J. Mariconda [S. T. Joshi, *I Am Providence: The Life and Times of H. P. Lovecraft*]; The Men Behind the Curtain, by Matt Cardin [Thomas Ligotti, *The Conspiracy against the Human Race*; H. P. Lovecraft, *Against Religion*]; Ramsey Campbell, Probably: The Missing Bits; What If Cthulhu Won?, by Martin Andersson [Darrell Schweitzer, ed., *Cthulhu's Reign*]; Shock or Schlock?, by Hank Wagner [Joe R. Lansdale, *Sanctified and Chicken-Fried*; John Skipp and Cody Goodfellow, *Jake's Wake*]; Horror and Fantasy for the Impecunious, by S. T. Joshi [Michael Kelahan, ed., *The Screaming Skull*; Michael Kelahan, ed., *The End of the World*; Sir Arthur Conan Doyle, *The Horror of the Heights*; Washington Irving, *The Legend of Sleepy Hollow*; Bram Stoker, *Dracula's Guest*; Oscar Wilde, *The Picture of Dorian Gray*]; A Werewolf Story with (Sharp) Teeth, by Robert Butterfield [Tom Fletcher, *The Leaping*]; Writing Above the Zombie Line, by Vicky Gilpin [Darrell Schweitzer and Martin H. Greenberg, ed.,

Full Moon City; Scott Edelman, *What Will Come After*]; Nutrition for the Dead, by Leigh Blackmore [Chris Lane, *Zombies: A Record of the Year of Infection*]; The United States of the Undead, by John Edgar Browning [Robin Becker, *Brains: A Zombie Memoir*]; Two Anthologies, 45 Stories, by Richard Bleiler [Ellen Datlow, ed., *Darkness: Two Decades of Modern Horror*; Stephen Jones, ed., *The Mammoth Book of the Best of Best New Horror*]; A Broad Range of Strange, by Jonathan Johnson [Jonathan Thomas, *Tempting Providence*]; Darkness with Depth, by Robert Butterfield [Maurice Broaddus and Jerry Gordon, ed., *Dark Faith*]; What Lurks in the Dark, by Van P. Viator [Alyson Hagy, *Ghosts of Wyoming*; Daniel McGachey, *They That Dwell in Dark Places*]; New Writers, New Horror, by John Edgar Browning [Jeani Rector, ed., *And Now the Nightmare Begins: The Horror Zine*]; Dante of the Dead, by Matt Cardin [Kim Paffenroth. *Valley of the Dead: The Truth Behind Dante's Inferno*]; Sympathy for Ig, by John Langan [Joe Hill, *Horns*]; Living in London Is Overrated, by Andy Trevathan [Tim Lebbon, *30 Days of Night: Fear of the Dark*]; A Ghost Melodrama, by June Pulliam [Simon Clark, *Ghost Monster*]; What If?, by Antoinette Winstead [Tananarive Due, *Blood Colony*]; Murder Most Macabre, by Tony Fonseca [Joe R. Lansdale, *The Bottoms*]; The Weird Scholar, by S. T. Joshi; Capsule Reviews.

83.   JOSEPH S. PULVER, SR. *Sin & Ashes.* 2010. 325 pp.

Contents. Death's Head Blues, by Laird Barron; Love Her Madly; She's Waiting . . .; *First There Is a Mountain . . . Then*; In This Desert Even the Air Burns; Even Night; Crow in Trick Town; When the Deal Goes Down; Devil's Got the Walkin' Blues; Dead 'Round Here Tonight; The Delirium of a Worm-Wizard; As the Sun Still Burns Away; Caligari, Again; Long-Stemmed Ghost Words; When the Moon Comes to Call; After Reading Michaux's "In the Land of Magic"; The Walking Man Walks; Silent No Longer; The Maiden of the Pines; Last Year in Carcosa; Scarlet Obeisance; Rendezvous Under Shadow Bridge; in front of an empty house in dead city; Ain't No Love on the Street; Perfect Grace; Kynothrabian Dirge; The Exorcism of Iagsat; Lonesome Separate Ways; Just Another Desert Night with Blood; After Death; I Often Dream of Words; Forever Changes; In the White Walls of Silence; Mother Stands for Comfort; Blow Wind Blow; 8's & Aces; A One-Way Fare; Don't Look Back; Long is the way and hard . . .; huddled in rags in a Kingsport alley . . .; Dead Ends and Empties; Sharp Fangs + Blood = Murder; Saint Nicholas Hall; Funeral in a Hate Field; An Orange Tick-Tick-Tick- Tick-Tick; Engravings; The Last Few Nights in a Life of Frost; Epilogue for Two Voices; To Live and Die in Arkham; The Last Twenty Miles of Wandering Again; Acknowledgments.

Notes: Cover art by J. Karl Bogartte. A second collection of horrific, fantastic, and surrealistic fiction by Pulver, following on his well-received first collection (see item 67).

84. FRED PHILLIPS. *From the Cauldron.* 2010. 132 pp.

Contents. THE FAIR FOLK: The Fair Folk; Metamorphosis; Giliniel; Sleep; De la Marche; One More; The Little Stone; Fleeting Hours; Frederick of Holland; On the Heath; Madrigal to Dian Alene; A Winter Night's Sleep; The Old Tavern; Ode to Asbjorn Gustavsson Haarfagr; Final Quest; Bane of Aeacus; The Gathering of Clan Creachain; The Formula; The Tale of the Scribe; Burleycon 1973; Chanson de Guerre; The Printed Grail; The Inn at the Side of the Road; The Mask; Yesudai; The Honour of Princes; Moira; They Also Rule, Who Only Stand and Baste; The Ballad of the Four Sons; Aisling for Mary Radich; Sonnet LIII. R.E.H. Style #3; Quest; Stand or Fall; The Price of Blood; Tiresias; WEIGHED IN THE SCALES: Origin; Ephemera; Chagrin; Sortilege; A Fragrance; Apathy; Futility; Damozel Alayne; Epitaph on an Unknown Howe in the Foothills of Wales; The Poet to His Bed; Angelique Perdue; Rendezvous; Toilette d'Angelique; Meistersang; At the Inn; Samhain; A Peek at Dürer; Discovery; Wrapped in Fabrics Red; Weighed in the Scales; To Clark Ashton Smith; Conundrum; Anomaly; Raw, New Things; PHANTASMS: The Pathways of the Dead; The Lost Legend of Ingoldsby; A Lovecraftian's Eye-View of Kipling; The Elder Ones; The Lost City; The Book; Janandra; Predecessors; Buried Truths; Caveat; The Presence; The Codex; Outpost; Somnambulist; Witness; A Lovecraftian Reads Caesar Midnight on Hallowe'en; Silent Watchers; The Shop; The Steeple; Recompense; Chiaroscuro; Impasse; Volte-Face; The Sword; Pale Visitor; The House; The Street; Wyckham; Phantasm; Erato; The Wanderer; The Donjon; Rubaiyat of Rub al-Khali; The Journey; Off the Beaten Track; The Pit; The Keep; The Travelers.

Notes. Cover illustration by Howard Wandrei. A distinctive collection of weird and fantastic poetry by Phillips, an elder statesman in the world of Lovecraftian and fantasy fandom.

85. S. T. JOSHI, EDITOR. *A Weird Writer in Our Midst: Early Criticism of H. P. Lovecraft.* 2010. 264 pp.

Contents: Introduction, by S. T. Joshi; I. RECOLLECTIONS OF LOVECRAFT: Howard P. Lovecraft [1890–1937], by Walter J. Coates; Amateur Affairs, by Hyman Bradofsky; [Letter to the Editor], by Robert Bloch; Interlude with Lovecraft, by Stuart M. Boland; Howard Phillips Lovecraft, by Muriel E. Eddy; I Met Lovecraft, by Paul Livingston Keil; The Man Who

Came at Midnight, by Ruth M. Eddy; II. CRITICISM IN LOVECRAFT'S LIFETIME: A Note on Howard P. Lovecraft's Verse, by Rheinhart Kleiner; Howard P. Lovecraft's Fiction, by W. Paul Cook; The Vivisector, by Zoilus [Alfred Galpin]; Preface to *The Shunned House*, by Frank Belknap Long, Jr.; A Weird Writer Is in Our Midst, by Vrest Orton; The Sideshow, by B. K. Hart; What Makes a Story Click?, by J. Randle Luten; III. COMMENTS FROM READERS; IV. CRITICISM FROM THE FAN WORLD: H. P. Lovecraft, Outsider, by August Derleth; A Master of the Macabre, by August Derleth; Disbelievers Ever, by R. W. Sherman; The Last of H. P. Lovecraft, by J. B. Michel; What of H. P. Lovecraft? or, A Commentary upon J. B. Michel, by Autolycus; H. P. Lovecraft: Strange Weaver, by J. Chapman Miske; Lovecraft and Benefit Street, by Dorothy Walter; [Letters to the Editor], by Thomas Ollive Mabbott; A Plea for Lovecraft, by W. Paul Cook; Let's All Jump on H.P.L., by P. Schuyler Miller; Howard Phillips Lovecraft, by Michael Harrison; The Lovecraft Cult, by Arthur F. Hillman; Lovecraft Is 86, by Francis T. Laney; Rusty Chains, by John Brunner; Some Notes on HPL, by Sam Moskowitz, Fritz Leiber, Edward Wood, and John Brunner; V. NOTICES FROM THE LITERARY COMMUNITY: Mystery and Adventure, by Will Cuppy; Horror Story Author Published by Fellow Writers, by Anonymous; [Review of *The Outsider and Others*], by T. O. Mabbott; Such Pulp as Dreams Are Made On, by Robert Allerton Parker; Macabre, Lyrical and Weird, by Peter De Vries; Mystery and Adventure, by Will Cuppy; Nightmare in Cthulu, by William Poster; Books Alive, by Vincent Starrett; Bookman's Holiday, by Charles Collins; Mystery and Adventure, by Will Cuppy; Poesque Doodles, by Marjorie Farber; Books Alive, by Vincent Starrett; The Phoenix Nest, by William Rose Benét; [Review of *Supernatural Horror in Literature*], by Fred Lewis Pattee; Pilgrims through Space and Time, by J. O. Bailey; Imagination Runs Wild, by Richard B. Gehman; Books Alive, by Vincent Starrett; A Bookman's Notebook, by Joseph Henry Jackson; Sabbat-Night Reading, by E. O. D. Keown; Of Good and Evil, by [Anthony Powell]; The Genius Who Lived Backwards, by Vincent H. Gaddis; APPENDIX: Some Vignettes; Notes; Index.

Notes. Cover illustration by Jason Eckhardt. An extensive collection of criticism of Lovecraft—early articles in the amateur and fan press, readers' comments from *Weird Tales* and *Astounding Stories*, and reviews in magazines and newspapers—charting Lovecraft's emergence from a pulp writer to an established literary figure.

Index of Authors, Editors, and Artists

Numbers refer to item, not to page.

HIPPOCAMPUS PRESS derives its name from H. P. Lovecraft's term of address (used thrice), in unpublished parts of letters to Frank Belknap Long, of which the following (from 6 April 1923) is representative: "be a nice little amethystine hippocampus, write your Old Grandpa, and prepare to visit Providentia's sequester'd shades when the sun is warm and genial."

Lightning Source UK Ltd.
Milton Keynes UK
04 April 2011

170344UK00001B/89/P